EQ Blueprint

Navigating Emotions for Resilience and Connection

Elena Santiago

Table of Contents

INTRODUCTION

One skill that is frequently ignored but extremely important is emotional intelligence (EQ). In a world where the pace of life seems to quicken with each passing day, where the demands of job, relationships, and personal development may sometimes feel overwhelming, there is one skill that jumps out as being particularly important. Welcome to "EQ Blueprint: Navigating Emotions for Resilience and Connection."

Emotional intelligence is the foundation of our capacity to comprehend and control our own feelings, as well as to empathize with the feelings of other people without losing our own. It is the compass that leads us across the complicated landscape of human interactions, assisting us in developing more profound connections and navigating adversities with grace and resiliency. Within the pages of this book, we set out on an adventure to investigate the intricacies of emotional intelligence, illuminating the significance of this trait in both our interpersonal and professional lives.

Beginning with self-awareness, which serves as the foundation upon which all other parts of emotional intelligence are constructed, we will delve into the essential components of emotional intelligence across the course of these pages. Following that, we will embark on a voyage through the realms of self-regulation, empathy, social skills, and motivation, during which we will discover practical tactics and activities to enhance each component of our emotional intelligence arsenal.

This book, however, is more than simply a theoretical investigation; it is a practical guide for individuals who are looking to improve their emotional intelligence (EQ) and acquire a deeper awareness of both themselves and about other people. Each chapter provides tangible ideas and real-world applications that are designed to inspire growth and connection. These include mastering the art of active listening and developing our ability to manage emotions during times of stress.

Whether you are an experienced leader who is wanting to inspire your team with empathy and authenticity or an individual who is striving to manage the intricacies of human interactions with grace and resilience, "EQ Blueprint" gives the roadmap you need to succeed in a world that is becoming increasingly linked.

Join me as we embark on this adventure that will revolutionize our lives; a journey that will lead to increased self-awareness, strengthened relationships, and a deeper comprehension of what it means to be really emotionally intelligent.

CHAPTER I

Understanding Emotional Intelligence

What is Emotional Intelligence?

Over the course of the last few decades, the idea of emotional intelligence (EI), which is often referred to as emotional quotient (EQ), has led to a substantial transformation in our understanding of human intellect and the dynamics of interpersonal relationships. Emotional intelligence (EI) comprises the more subtle parts of human behavior that require detecting, understanding, managing, and effectively using emotions in both oneself and others. This is in contrast to standard measurements of intelligence, such as intelligence quotient (IQ), which focus on cognitive abilities including logic and reasoning. The relevance of emotional abilities in personal success, social connections, and professional situations is brought to light by this more comprehensive view of intelligence.

Self-awareness and self-management, and also social awareness and relationship management, are at the heart of emotional intelligence. Emotional intelligence is a key competency. Through the interplay of these components, humans are able to manage the intricacies of emotional responses and social interactions with dexterity and empathy. The notion of emotional intelligence (EI) has its origins in psychology research, where it was discovered to be a significant component that differentiates persons who achieve in many life areas despite having similar levels of cognitive intelligence among themselves.

Self-awareness, the first pillar of emotional intelligence, is characterized by a keen awareness of one's own feelings, as well as one's own strengths, flaws, values, and motivations. Individuals are able to notice how their sentiments might influence their ideas and actions, and how these, in turn, affect their relationships and their performance at work because of their ability for introspection. An individual who possesses a high level of self-awareness is able to comprehend their own unique triggers and effectively control their emotional responses to a variety of situations. This, in turn, leads to more deliberate decision-making and an increase in their own personal efficacy.

The ability to regulate and redirect disruptive emotions and impulses is referred to as self-management or self-regulation. Self-awareness serves as the basis with which self-management or self-regulation is built. Keeping one's composure in the face of adversity, adjusting to new circumstances without difficulty, and overcoming obstacles with fortitude are all essential. When it comes to maintaining professionalism in the workplace, cultivating solid personal relationships, and accomplishing long-term goals, effective self-regulation is absolutely necessary. Individuals are able to engage in reflective thinking prior to taking action and to make decisions that are relevant with their objectives and principles.

One further essential aspect of emotional intelligence is social awareness, which refers to the ability to comprehend the feelings, requirements, and worries of other individuals, to identify and respond appropriately to emotional signs, and to feel at ease in social situations. One of its components is empathy, which can be defined as the capacity to see and comprehend the viewpoints and emotions of other people, even when those emotions are not directly communicated consciously. The ability to empathize with others is an essential skill for leadership, cooperation, and any other form of interpersonal engagement since it enables deeper connections and exchanges to take place.

As a last point of discussion, relationship management, which is frequently regarded as the most obvious facet of emotional intelligence, encompasses the capacity to motivate, influence, and cultivate others while simultaneously effectively managing disagreement. In order to enhance communication, leadership, and teamwork, it is dependent on the deployment of the other components of emotional intelligence in social settings in an efficient manner. People who have great relationship management abilities are adept at constructing and maintaining networks of personal and professional relationships that are healthy and supportive of one another.

Beyond the realm of personal growth, the relevance of emotional intelligence should not be underestimated. In the field of education, it has resulted in the development of curriculum that are intended to improve students' emotional intelligence (EI) skills, so preparing them for more successful relationships with other people and for improved emotional well-being. The concept of emotional intelligence (EI) is becoming more recognized in the workplace as a critical driver of leadership effectiveness, team performance, and organizational productivity. Leaders that possess a high emotional intelligence are better able to engage their colleagues, handle the intricacies of organizational change, and create a good work atmosphere that encourages innovation and resilience.

Furthermore, the idea of emotional intelligence has major implications for one's mental health. When an individual is able to comprehend and control their feelings, it can result in an enhancement of their psychological well-being and a reduction in the occurrence of mental health problems such as anxiety and depression. Through this, individuals are given the ability to confront the problems of life with a more positive perspective and to cultivate relationships that are more satisfying and supportive.

The process of developing emotional intelligence is an ongoing one, one that requires continuous learning and practice with the goal of achieving the desired results. EI, on the other hand, can be developed and improved over time by activities such as self-reflection, mindfulness, empathy exercises, and practical application in everyday interactions. This is in contrast to IQ, which tends to remain relatively steady over one's lifetime. It is not just that this growing process increases the well-being and effectiveness of individuals, but it also contributes to the development of a society that is more emotionally intelligent and empathic.

In conclusion, emotional intelligence is a multidimensional idea that revolutionizes our perception of what it means to be intelligent due to its many facets. Self-awareness, self-regulation, social awareness, as well as relationship management are some of the essential emotional and social abilities that are required for success in life. It incorporates all of these talents. The significance of emotional intelligence extends beyond the realm of individual accomplishment, as it has an impact on educational processes, workplace dynamics, the development of leadership skills, and mental health. It is becoming increasingly important for persons who want to lead lives that are more meaningful, effective, and connected to others to work on developing their emotional intelligence. This is because we are continuing to acknowledge and respect the importance that emotions play in our lives. When we live in a world that frequently places an emphasis on intellectual accomplishments, the emphasis placed on emotional intelligence serves as a reminder of the significant influence that our feelings and the relationships we have with other people have on our overall success and pleasure.

Importance of Emotional Intelligence in personal and professional life

A potent predictor of success in both personal and professional spheres, the idea of emotional intelligence (EI), also called emotional quotient (EQ), has emerged as a powerful indicator of success. It transcends the standard measurements of intelligence, such as intelligence quotient (IQ). In the context of oneself and in connection to other people, emotional intelligence (EI) refers to the capacity to identify, comprehend, control, and make effective use of one's emotions. This complex capability is becoming more acknowledged as a significant predictor of human well-being, relationship satisfaction, the efficacy of leadership, and the productivity of organizations. It is possible to navigate the complexities of human emotions and interactions with the help of a comprehensive framework that is offered by emotional intelligence, which is an important trait that is applicable to every facet of life.

When it comes to one's personal life, emotional intelligence creates the groundwork for a multitude of beneficial outcomes, such as improved psychological health, increased relationship satisfaction, and enhanced abilities to resolve conflicts. The component of emotional intelligence known as self-awareness is at the core of these advantages. Self-awareness enables individuals to develop an understanding of their own emotional states and to notice the ways in which these emotions influence their thoughts and behaviors. This understanding is essential for self-regulation because it enables individuals to effectively manage their emotions, even when confronted with difficult circumstances. As a result, the occurrence of impulsive reactions is reduced, and answers that are more considered are made possible.

In addition, emotional intelligence makes a substantial contribution to the formation and maintenance of relationships that are both helpful and healthy amongst individuals. Empathy is known as a fundamental aspect of emotional intelligence (EI), which enables individuals to comprehend and identify with the feelings of other people, hence establishing a sense of connection and mutual respect. The cultivation of strong, meaningful relationships that are marked by open communication and mutual support is greatly aided by this understanding of empathy. Individuals who possess effective social skills are able to handle social situations with ease, which in turn enhances their capacity to construct and maintain a large network of personal relationships. Effective social skills are another facet of emotional intelligence.

There is no doubt that the value of emotional intelligence is as significant when it comes to the professional setting. Technical abilities and cognitive ability are not enough to ensure success in today's workplace, which is characterized by a high rate of change and a diverse workforce. Leadership, teamwork, customer interactions, and flexibility to change are all areas in which emotional intelligence plays a crucial role. Leaders that possess a high level of emotional intelligence are skilled at inspiring and motivating their people, thereby establishing an atmosphere of trust and collaboration that is the driving force behind the success of their organizations. These kind of leaders are adept at identifying the emotional needs of their staff members, addressing concerns in a compassionate manner, and cultivating a constructive work culture that boosts employee engagement and productivity.

The ability of individuals to effectively collaborate with coworkers who come from a variety of backgrounds and personalities is another way in which emotional intelligence contributes to the improvement of collaboration. By constructively managing conflicts, communicating effectively, and empathizing with the perspectives of others, individuals of a team who have a high emotional intelligence (EI) contributed to the creation of a pleasant working environment. When it comes to accomplishing collective objectives and successfully navigating the intricacies of organizational tasks, the dynamic of a team that is cooperative and helpful is absolutely essential.

In addition, emotional intelligence is necessary for effectively managing client connections and providing service. When professionals have a high emotional intelligence, they are better able to comprehend and respond to the feelings and requirements of their customers, which eventually leads to increased customer satisfaction as well as loyalty. In today's highly competitive business environment, where positive customer experiences may have a huge impact on a company's reputation as well as its bottom line, the ability to connect with customers on an emotional level is a vital differentiator that will set you apart from the competition.

When it comes to circumstances involving organizational change and uncertainty, the adaptability component of emotional intelligence is very important to consider. People who have a high emotional intelligence capacity are more robust and flexible, able to effectively manage stress, and able to traverse the challenges of change while maintaining a good attitude. The individual not only reaps the benefits of this resilience by boosting their personal well-being and job satisfaction, but it also contributes to the organization's capacity to adapt and thrive in the face of changing circumstances.

Traditional education and professional training programs frequently fail to adequately address the concept of emotional intelligence, despite the fact that it is of the utmost significance. Due to the fact that this void has been identified, numerous companies and educational institutions are currently implementing EI development into their education programs and training activities.

Individuals and organizations are able to realize their full potential and acquire greater levels of success if they begin cultivating emotional intelligence at a young age and continue to develop it throughout their careers.

In conclusion, the significance of emotional intelligence in both one's personal life and one's professional life cannot be emphasized. When it comes to personal situations, emotional intelligence is essential to the psychological well-being, the quality of relationships, and the successful resolution of conflicts. Effective leadership, teamwork, customer satisfaction, and the ability to adapt to change are all directly correlated to this trait in the professional world. The global landscape is always shifting, and as a result, there is a growing emphasis on social and emotional abilities. As a result, emotional intelligence is becoming an increasingly important factor in determining success and fulfillment. An investment in the development of emotional intelligence is not only a path to personal and professional progress, but it is also an essential step toward the construction of a society that is more empathic, understanding, and productive.

Components of Emotional Intelligence: Self-awareness, self-regulation, empathy, social skills, motivation

In the 1990s, psychologists came up with the term "emotional intelligence," which has since become an essential component in comprehending human behavior and the ways in which people interact with one another. Emotional intelligence (EI) is known as the capacity to identify, comprehend, control, and make good use of one's own and other people's feelings and emotions. Self-awareness, self-regulation, empathy, social skills, and motivation are the five essential components that have been broken down. This idea has been broken down completely. The development of emotional intelligence, the improvement of interpersonal relationships, and the achievement of success in a variety of facets of life are all built upon these components, which serve as the basis.

With regard to emotional intelligence, self-awareness is the foundational component. Emotional intelligence is known as the capacity of an individual to comprehend their own feelings, strengths, shortcomings, and ideals, as well as the ways in which these aspects influence their thoughts and behaviors. A person who possesses a high level of self-awareness is not only aware of the emotional state that they are experiencing at any given moment, but they are also aware of the impact that their feelings have on other people. As a result of this awareness, individuals are able to detect the emotional triggers that they experience and comprehend how they react to different situations. This awareness is essential for personal development. Through the cultivation of self-awareness, individuals are able to make decisions that are more informed, strengthen their relationships, and handle the challenges that life presents with greater ease and increased confidence.

The ability to govern and control one's emotions and impulses is referred to as self-regulation, which is a subset of self-awareness. People who are skilled in self-regulation are able to adjust to shifting conditions, deal with stress in a productive manner, and resist the desire to engage in impulsive activity. Due to the fact that it helps individuals to think before acting and to preserve their standards of honesty and integrity even when confronted with challenging circumstances, self-regulation is an essential component of both personal and professional success. When it comes to creating a pleasant and productive environment, possessing this aspect of emotional intelligence is vital, not only for oneself but also for people who are in their immediate vicinity.

The third component of emotional intelligence is empathy, which goes beyond simple pity toward another person. It requires putting oneself in the position of another person, empathizing with them, and responding with compassion and sensitivity. It also requires understanding and sharing the sentiments of other people. As a result of its ability to facilitate more effective communication and the formation of more profound connections with other people, empathy is an essential feature in the process of constructing robust and healthy relationships. The ability to empathize with others is beneficial to leadership and teamwork in professional contexts because it enables individuals to comprehend the various points of view and emotional reactions of their coworkers. This, in turn, helps to cultivate a more welcoming and encouraging atmosphere throughout the workplace.

An array of interpersonal abilities, such as effective communication, conflict resolution, leadership, and the ability to develop and sustain relationships, are included in the fourth component, which is referred to as social skills. The ability to navigate social situations, positively influence others, and work together towards common goals are all qualities that are possessed by those who have excellent social skills. As a result of their ability to contribute to the development of trust, the constructive resolution of disagreements, and the creation of a healthy social milieu, these abilities are necessary in both personal and professional settings. The ability to apply one's self-awareness, self-regulation, and empathy in real-world encounters is reflected in a person's social skills, which are often the outer manifestation of a person's emotional intelligence.

On a final note, motivation, which is an essential component of emotional intelligence, is the internal drive that propels individuals toward the accomplishment of their objectives. In contrast to extrinsic motivation, which is motivated by incentives from the outside world, intrinsic motivation is driven by the desire to improve oneself and the joy that comes from achieving personal goals. People who are highly motivated are able to bounce back from setbacks, maintain a positive outlook, and remain dedicated to their own personal and professional growth. As a result of their relentless attempts to achieve their goals, they perceive problems as possibilities for progress and view them as opportunities for growth. Individuals are motivated to pursue their passions and endure in the face of hardship when they possess this element of emotional intelligence, which is essential for both personal fulfillment as well as professional success.

Complex and ever-changing is the dynamic interaction that takes place between these five components of emotional intelligence. The cornerstone is self-awareness, which in turn enables individuals to notice and comprehend their feelings, as well as the ways in which those feelings influence their conduct and their interactions with other people. The ability to self-regulate enables individuals to effectively manage their feelings, which in turn makes it possible for them to react to situations in a manner that is both balanced and helpful.

With the ability to connect with others on a deeper level, manage social difficulties, and develop strong, supportive relationships, empathy and social skills are essential for successful interpersonal interactions. This is because they enable individuals to connect with others on a deeper level. Last but not least, motivation is what gives one the drive and the perseverance that are necessary to pursue goals and triumph over obstacles.

Given the current state of affairs, it is impossible to overestimate the significance of emotional intelligence. Emotional intelligence (EI) is beneficial to one's mental and emotional health, as well as to the quality of one's relationships and to the process of personal development. When it comes to the professional world, it is a significant factor that identifies the efficacy of leadership, the cohesiveness of teams, and the overall performance of organizations. Leaders who have a high level of emotional intelligence are able to have the ability to inspire and encourage their colleagues, effectively manage conflicts, and cultivate a favorable work culture that increases both productivity and job satisfaction respectively. Furthermore, emotional intelligence is essential for successfully navigating the intricacies of a world that is becoming increasingly linked and rapidly changing. In this world, the capacity to comprehend and control one's emotions is essential for both success and well-being.

In conclusion, the components of emotional intelligence, which include self-awareness, self-regulation, empathy, social skills, and motivation, are necessary for comprehending and managing emotions, establishing and maintaining healthy relationships, and attaining success in both one's personal and professional life. These are not innate abilities; rather, they are able to be cultivated and improved over time via consistent practice and self-dedication. Individuals can improve their capacity to handle the challenges that life presents, cultivate meaningful connections with others, and realize their full potential if they make an investment in the development of their emotional intelligence. It is becoming increasingly obvious that emotional intelligence is not merely a collection of talents but rather a way of life that places an emphasis on empathy, understanding, and personal development. This realization comes about as the relevance of EI continues to be acknowledged and respected in all aspects of life.

The science behind Emotional Intelligence

From the traditional limitations of cognitive skills to the world of emotional and social competences, the investigation of emotional intelligence (EI) represents a major movement in the understanding of human intelligence. This shift will allow for the expansion of the scope of intelligence beyond the traditional boundaries. This change highlights the realization that success in life is not just dependent on intellectual talents but also on how individuals manage their emotions, traverse the intricacies of social situations, and make personal decisions that result in positive consequences. Emotional intelligence (EI) is a field of study that investigates the neurological, psychological, and social systems that drive these skills. This field of study provides insights into how EI develops, how it functions, and how it affects our lives.

On a neurological level, emotional intelligence may be traced back to the limbic system of the brain, which is the part of the brain that is in charge of memory as well as emotions. The prefrontal cortex, which is the part of the brain that is involved in planning, decision-making, and the regulation of social conduct, collaborates with the limbic system to help regulate social behavior. One of the most important aspects of emotional regulation is the interaction between the limbic system and the prefrontal cortex. This interaction enables humans to react to emotional inputs in a manner that is both deliberate and constructive. It has been demonstrated via research in the field of neuroscience that the development of certain brain regions and the connectivity between them has a substantial impact in an individual's ability for emotional intelligence. This capacity influences how emotions are processed, comprehended, and how they are regulated.

From a psychological point of view, emotional intelligence refers to a collection of skills that enable individuals to recognize, assimilate, comprehend, and control their feelings and emotions. The Mayer-Salovey model, which is considered to be one of the foundational frameworks in the field of emotional intelligence research, classifies these abilities into four distinct domains. These domains include the ability to precisely perceive emotions in oneself as well as others, the ability to utilize emotions to facilitate thinking, the ability to comprehend emotional meanings and the relationships between different emotions, and the capacity to manage emotions in order to foster emotional and intellectual development. Individuals who have higher degrees of emotional intelligence have been shown to have superior mental health, work performance, and leadership skills, according to research conducted in the field of psychology. Based on these findings, it emerges that emotional intelligence (EI) plays a significant part in both personal well-being and professional success, effectively moderating the connection between emotions and a variety of life outcomes.

When it comes to society, emotional intelligence is an essential component in the process of establishing and sustaining personal and professional connections. For efficient communication and the settlement of conflicts, it is vital to possess the ability to empathize with other people, to comprehend social signs, and to constructively regulate interactions with other people. study conducted in the field of social psychology has shed light on the significance of emotional intelligence (EI) in social perception and behavior. This study has demonstrated that persons who possess a high EI are better able to navigate social difficulties, construct networks, and cultivate meaningful connections. Having this level of social competence not only improves personal relationships, but it also makes a contribution to the dynamics of teams and the culture of organizations, highlighting the importance of emotional intelligence across a wide variety of social settings.

The development of emotional intelligence is influenced by a number of factors, including those that are genetic, environmental, and educational in nature. Although there is a possibility that certain components of emotional intelligence, such as the capacity to recognize emotions, are influenced by genetics, environmental factors, such as the dynamics of the family, the relationships with other people, and the cultural background, have a key role in the development of emotional and social abilities. Furthermore, it has been demonstrated that educational programs that place an emphasis on social and emotional learning (SEL) are able to boost Emotional Intelligence in children and adolescents. This suggests that EI is something that can be acquired and enhanced over the course of time. The development of emotional intelligence (EI) competences, which are essential for achieving success in life, is fostered by these programs, which place an emphasis on self-awareness, emotional regulation, empathy, social skills, and responsible decision-making.

Studies have linked high EI to a number of good impacts, including improved mental health, increased academic and professional accomplishment, and higher levels of pleasure in relationships. The influence of Emotional Intelligence on life outcomes has been a key topic of research, and studies have linked high EI to these positive consequences. To give one example, people who have a high EI are more capable of dealing with stressful situations and difficult circumstances, which in turn reduces the risk that they may have mental health problems such as anxiety and depression. There is a correlation between emotional intelligence (EI) and effective leadership, teamwork, and conflict management in the workplace. This leads to improved organizational performance and increased employee satisfaction. The capacity for empathy and understanding that is inherent in emotional intelligence also makes it easier to form deeper and more meaningful connections with other people, which in turn enriches both personal relationships and social interactions.

The idea of emotional intelligence has been subjected to criticism and skepticism, particularly with regard to its measurement and ways in which it differs from other types of intelligence and personality traits. This is the case despite the significant research that has been conducted to demonstrate the significance of emotional intelligence. The existing measures of emotional intelligence, which include anything from self-report questionnaires to ability-based exams, have been criticised for their potential inability to adequately capture the complexities of emotional and social competencies. Furthermore, there are academics who dispute the amount of overlap that exists between emotional intelligence (EI) and personality variables such as agreeableness and conscientiousness, implying that EI might not be a singular concept. In response, advocates of emotional intelligence (EI) highlight the empirical data that links EI to certain outcomes and argue for the ongoing refining of assessment tools and theoretical models in order to better understand and evaluate Emotional Intelligence (EI).

In conclusion, the scientific study of emotional intelligence comprises a multidisciplinary investigation into the ways in which humans detect, comprehend, manage, and make use of emotions in themselves and in others. Studies in the areas of psychology and social science investigate the abilities and competences that make up emotional intelligence (EI), as well as the impact that these talents and competencies have on both personal and professional life. Neuroscientific research sheds light on the brain mechanisms that underlie EI. There is an intricate interaction between genetic, environmental, and educational factors that shapes the development of emotional intelligence (EI). This interaction highlights the potential for growth and improvement in these essential skills. The corpus of research that supports the significance of emotional intelligence in achieving success in life is enormous, despite the fact that there are obstacles in measuring and conceptualizing it. This highlights the significance of continuing to investigate and comprehend this essential component of human intelligence.

CHAPTER II

The Foundation of Self-Awareness

Importance of self-awareness in Emotional Intelligence

In the field of emotional intelligence (EI), self-awareness is a cornerstone that plays a vital part in how individuals comprehend and manage their internal landscape of emotions, as well as how they interact within their external world. Self-awareness provides individuals with the ability to understand and navigate their own emotions. This essential aspect of emotional intelligence encompasses the capacity of individuals to perceive and comprehend their own feelings, motivations, strengths, shortcomings, and values, as well as the influence that their actions have on these aspects of themselves and others. It is impossible to emphasize the significance of self-awareness in relation to emotional intelligence. Self- awareness serves as the foundation upon which other aspects of EI, such as self-regulation, empathy, social skills, and motivation, are constructed and developed. This section examines the multidimensional significance of self-awareness in personal development, interpersonal interactions, decision-making, and leadership, highlighting the fundamental role that self-awareness plays in the process of achieving emotional and intellectual progress.

At the individual level, self-awareness makes it easier to gain a more profound comprehension of one's emotional reactions and triggers, which in turn enables people to manage their feelings in a more efficient manner.

Individuals who have a high level of self-awareness are able to understand the underlying causes of their feelings, differentiate between fleeting emotions and more fundamental thoughts, and select how to react to a variety of situations with better clarity and control. This is because they are able to recognize the complexities of their emotional experiences. This ability to reflect on oneself is essential for emotional regulation since it enables one to manage one's feelings in a manner that is constructive rather than destructive. People who are self- aware are better able to deal with stress, adjust to new circumstances, and face obstacles with resilience, all of which contribute to their overall mental and emotional well-being.

By increasing one's self-awareness, one can improve their ability to interact and connect with other people, which is important in the context of interpersonal relationships. The ability to comprehend one's feelings provides the way for the expression of feelings and requirements in a manner that is more lucid and efficient, hence creating communication that is both open and honest. Furthermore, self-awareness enables individuals to realize how their words and actions affect other people, which ultimately results in interactions that are more empathic and compassionate. Individuals are able to create relationships that are healthier, more helpful, and defined by mutual understanding and respect if they are cognizant of their emotional state and the influence that it has on their conduct.

The ability to make decisions is yet another domain in which self-awareness plays an exceptional role. Feelings have a huge impact on our decisions, and we frequently do so unintentionally. On the other hand, those who have a high level of self-awareness are able to recognize the emotional factors that influence the choices they make that they make. Because of this knowledge, they are able to differentiate between rational thought and emotional impulse, which ultimately results in decision-making that is more balanced and objective. When it comes to making judgments, whether in a personal or professional context, the capacity to make informed decisions that take into account both emotional and rational components is extremely essential. This ability can lead to outcomes that are more in line with one's ambitions and principles.

When it comes to good leadership, self-awareness is an absolutely necessary component. Leaders who have a great sense of self-awareness are aware of both their skills and their limitations, which enables them to make the most of their strengths and seek assistance when it is required. These types of leaders are also aware of their own emotional states and are aware of how their mood and actions influence the dynamics of the team as well as the morale of the members. This kind of self-awareness helps to cultivate authenticity, which in turn inspires trust and confidence among members of the team. In addition, leaders who are self-aware are in a better position to inspire and direct others, thereby establishing a constructive and fruitful working atmosphere that fosters growth, innovation, and collaboration.

Introspection, feedback, and a willingness to learn are all necessary components of the ongoing process of developing self-awareness, which is a process that is ongoing. Enhancing one's self-awareness can be accomplished through the use of techniques such as mindfulness meditation, journaling, and soliciting constructive criticism from others. These techniques can provide insights into one's emotional patterns and actions, as well as the impact that these patterns and behaviors have on one's life and the lives of others. This never-ending voyage of self-discovery not only contributes to the enhancement of one's personal and professional development, but it also helps to strengthen the other aspects of emotional intelligence, thereby establishing a positive cycling pattern of development and enhancement.

Self-awareness is a skill that, despite its tremendous benefits, can be difficult to cultivate since it requires one to confront unsettling realities about themselves and to accept vulnerability. The benefits of this activity, on the other hand, are substantial, as they result in enhanced emotional control, relationships that are more satisfying, greater decision-making, and enhanced leadership abilities. As a result, self-awareness is not only a component of emotional intelligence; rather, it is an essential component of living a life that is conscious, intentional, and rewarding.

In conclusion, self-awareness is a crucial element of emotional intelligence, as it serves as the basis upon which other aspects of EI are constructed. Its significance permeates every facet of one's personal and professional life, contributing to improvements in emotional well-being, interpersonal connections, decision-making, and leadership. Individuals are able to manage the complexities of their emotional experiences and the social world with better competence and grace if they cultivate their self-awareness. By doing so, individuals not only enjoy greater success in their personal and professional lives, but they also contribute to the development of societies that are more emotionally intelligent, sensitive, and understanding. It is a rewarding trip that offers vital insights and growth, highlighting the pivotal role that self-awareness plays in the development and use of emotional intelligence by demonstrating that the pursuit of self-awareness, despite its challenges, is a worthwhile path.

Techniques for developing self-awareness

The development of self-awareness is a crucial step on the path to personal development, development of emotional intelligence, and improvement of interpersonal interactions. Individuals are able to get an understanding of their ideas, feelings, strengths, and shortcomings, as well as the impact that their actions have on both other people and the environment, when they have self- awareness. It is a never-ending voyage of introspection and reflection that enables one to manage the difficulties of life with more ease and self-assurance. There are many different methods that may be utilized to aid the growth of self-awareness, and each of these methods provides a distinct perspective into the inner workings of one's mind and heart. Throughout this section, we will delve into these methods and investigate how they might help one gain a more profound awareness of themselves.

Mindfulness meditation is widely regarded as one of the most effective strategies for increasing one's level of self-awareness. One of the practices of mindfulness is paying attention to the here and now, noticing one's thoughts, feelings, and sensations without passing judgment on them. Mindfulness meditation, when practiced on a regular basis, can assist individuals in being more aware of their internal states as well as the complexities of their emotional responses. Because of this increased awareness, individuals are able to notice patterns in their thoughts and behaviors, which enables them to have a deeper comprehension of the emotional triggers that they experience and the ways in which they can more successfully handle those triggers. In addition, practicing mindfulness helps one become more accepting of themselves, which in turn cultivates a more sympathetic and understanding attitude toward one's own shortcomings and vulnerabilities.

Self-awareness can also be developed through the use of another powerful tool: journaling. Through the act of writing down one's thoughts, feelings, and experiences, one might gain significant insights into their own inner existence. It provides the opportunity to contemplate one's personal objectives, values, and beliefs, as well as the manner in which they are aligned with one's behaviors and choices. Additionally, keeping a journal can assist in tracking development over time, highlighting areas of growth as well as areas that require significant focus. The act of reviewing diary entries on a regular basis allows individuals to recognize patterns in their behavior and emotional responses, so developing a more profound comprehension of the factors that motivate their behaviors and the means by which they can make choices that are more conscious.

In order to develop one's own self-awareness, it is essential to receive feedback from other people. Through the process of soliciting and receiving feedback from friends, family members, coworkers, and mentors, one can gain an external perspective on their behavior and how it impacts the lives of others. The provision of constructive feedback affords individuals the chance to comprehend the disparities that exist between their own self-perception and the way in which others perceive them. This information from the outside can be quite helpful in identifying blind spots and places that provide room for improvement. Nevertheless, it is of the utmost importance to approach feedback with an open mind, as well as a willingness to ponder and examine it in a sincere manner, even if such critique may be difficult to hear.

Additionally, self-awareness can be increased through the use of personality tests and evaluations. The Myers-Briggs Type Indicator (MBTI), the Enneagram, and the StrengthsFinder are all examples of instruments that can be utilized to get a better understanding of an individual's personality characteristics, strengths, weaknesses, and preferred ways of interacting with the world. While it is important to remember that these evaluations should not be interpreted as definitive labels, they can be used as a jumping off point for introspection and comprehension. The framework that they provide allows for the investigation of personal tendencies and the ways in which these tendencies can impact one's professional and personal life. Nevertheless, it is of the utmost importance to make use of these tools as a component of a more comprehensive strategy for achieving self-awareness, incorporating their insights with personal reflection and feedback from other individuals.

Developing a sense of self-awareness can also be accomplished through the process of the setting and assessment of personal goals. The setting of goals provides individuals with a sense of purpose and direction, enabling them to match their activities with their values and aspirations. Individuals are able to monitor their progress and reflect on both their accomplishments and the areas in which they struggle when they establish objectives that are SMART, which stands for specific, measurable, attainable, relevant, and time-bound. This technique not only helps one become more self-aware, but it also has the potential to stimulate both personal and professional development. Making ensuring that one's objectives are in line with their ever-evolving awareness of themselves and their aspirations can be accomplished by regularly examining and modifying them based on self-reflection and feedback collected from others.

Increased self-awareness can also be achieved via the practice of mindful listening and communication. By engaging in active listening and communicating in an open and honest manner, individuals are encouraged to pay attention to their own thoughts and feelings, as well as the manner in which they express them. By taking a mindful approach to communication, one might become aware of patterns in their interactions, such as inclinations to react defensively, avoid conflict, or seek validation. By gaining an awareness of these patterns, individuals have the opportunity to concentrate on improving their communication skills, which can lead to relationships that are better and more meaningful.

For the final point, one of the most effective ways to cultivate self-awareness is to expose oneself to novel experiences and to venture outside of one's comfort zone. Individuals are forced to adapt and learn as a result of new experiences because they challenge their preconceived assumptions and their regular responses. Whether it's going on a trip, acquiring a new skill, or simply switching up one's daily routine, these kinds of experiences have the potential to offer new perspectives and insights about one's personality, preferences, and resilience. Self-reflection on personal development and adaptability is encouraged by them, which contributes to a more nuanced sense of one's own identity.

In conclusion, the process of developing self-awareness is a multi-faceted process that incorporates a range of strategies, each of which offers distinctive insights into the character of the individual. A deeper understanding of one's thoughts, feelings, and behaviors, as well as the impact they have on the world, can be achieved through the utilization of a variety of techniques, including but not limited to mindfulness meditation and journaling, seeking feedback, participating in personality assessments, establishing personal goals, practicing mindful communication, and welcoming new experiences. Individuals are able to start on a journey of self-discovery by incorporating these approaches into their daily lives, which ultimately results in increased emotional intelligence, enhanced relationships, and a life that is more satisfying. Commitment, openness, and a desire to confront and embrace the intricacies of the self are all necessary components of the path to self-awareness. However, the rewards of this journey are incalculable, as they offer a more profound and conscious experience of life.

Identifying personal strengths and weaknesses

One of the most important aspects of self-awareness and personal development is the process of determining one's own particular talents and weaknesses. Individuals are able to gain a better understanding of their capabilities, preferences, and areas in which they could develop through the process of introspection, which in turn promotes growth and achievement in a variety of aspects of life. Recognizing and capitalizing on one's talents while simultaneously acknowledging and working to improve one's flaws can result in a life that is more satisfying and productive on both a personal and professional level. The purpose of this section is to investigate the significance of recognizing one's own strengths and shortcomings, the approaches that may be taken to do this, and the influence that this comprehension has on one's own development and accomplishments.

Recognizing the abilities, skills, and characteristics that an individual excels at or feels particularly confident in is an essential aspect of an individual's process of understanding their strengths. The natural qualities and abilities that contribute to an individual's effectiveness in executing tasks, resolving problems, and navigating social relationships are referred to as strengths. Not only do they provide a sense of direction and confidence, but they also serve as the basis upon which success can be constructed. The process of identifying these qualities needs one to think back on previous achievements, solicit feedback from other people, and be conscious of the activities that bring about feelings of fulfillment and a sense of accomplishment. It is not an exercise in ego inflate to acknowledge one's personal qualities; rather, it is a recognition of one's distinctive contributions and an acknowledgment of one's potential for excellence.

On the other hand, recognizing those areas in which one may have difficulty or lack confidence is an essential part of identifying shortcomings. These are the qualities of a person's personality or skill set that have the potential to impair performance or lead to difficulties in personal relationships or personal aspirations in the professional world. Because it needs openness and a willingness to accept imperfection, confronting shortcomings is frequently more difficult than celebrating positives. This is because it requires a desire to accept. Recognizing one's shortcomings, on the other hand, is an essential component of personal development since it reveals problematic areas in which concentrated effort and improvement can result in significant growth and improved performance.

Identifying one's own particular strengths and shortcomings can be accomplished through a variety of approaches. An strategy that involves a conscious and honest evaluation of one's feelings, behaviors, and reactions in a variety of situations is sometimes referred to as self-reflection. This is likely the most straightforward method. In order to emphasize strengths, it is helpful to reflect on moments of success and satisfaction. On the other hand, analyzing occasions of hardship or failure may show flaws through reflection. Within the context of this process, journaling may be a very useful tool since it offers a space for continuous self-exploration and the monitoring of changes over time.

Receiving feedback from other people is another important strategy that may be used to determine one's strengths and limitations. Friends, family members, coworkers, and mentors are all examples of people who can provide an outsider's perspective on their capabilities and difficulties. This input, particularly when it is constructive and offered with care, has the potential to provide insights that might not be obvious through self-reflection alone. When attempting to obtain a full understanding of one's own strengths and flaws, it is essential to solicit input from an array of relevant sources.

As well as providing useful insights into one's strengths and limitations, personality tests and professional evaluations can also be of great assistance. A organized understanding of one's personality traits, preferences, and possible areas for improvement can be obtained through the use of instruments such as the Myers-Briggs Type Indicator, StrengthsFinder, or the Enneagram. Performance reviews and 360-degree feedback are two examples of professional assessments that can be used to identify strengths and deficiencies in a work environment. These evaluations can also serve as a foundation for career development and progress.

Understanding one's own talents and shortcomings, once they have been determined, has a significant impact on the development of one's own life. Individuals are able to flourish in areas where they naturally perform well when they capitalize on their strengths, which results in increased engagement, contentment, and potential for success. It gives people the ability to make strategic decisions regarding their employment, relationships, and personal ambitions, allowing them to line their paths with the natural talents and capabilities they possess. The practice of concentrating on one's strengths can not only increase one's self-assurance and resilience, but it can also provide a strong basis for overcoming obstacles and failures.

Taking steps to improve one's weaknesses, on the other hand, is a gateway to personal development and education. Individuals are able to create specific goals for progress, seek out resources and assistance, and accept problems as chances for growth when they acknowledge the areas in which they are having difficulty. It is possible to develop a more well-rounded skill set, higher adaptability, and increased empathy for others who are experiencing struggles that are comparable to your own by working on your deficiencies. To be successful, one must have a growth mindset, which is known as the conviction that one can change and improve through the application of work and dedication.

A dynamic and continuing process, assessing one's strengths and shortcomings and working with them is a process that is carried out in practice. Continuously evaluating oneself, actively seeking and incorporating feedback, and adapting to new possibilities and difficulties are all required components of this process. Additionally, it is necessary to strike a balance between concentrating on one's talents in order to maximize potential and correcting one's deficiencies in order to minimize limits. This well-rounded approach helps to cultivate a holistic perspective on human development, in which success is not just about excelling in particular domains but also about growing and improving in all facets of one's life.

In conclusion, one of the most important steps in the process of developing one's self-awareness and personal growth is to recognize one's own personal strengths and shortcomings. This enables individuals to gain an understanding of their own strengths and weaknesses, which in turn helps them make decisions regarding their employment, relationships, and personal objectives. Individuals are able to get insights into their strengths and limitations through the process of self-reflection, feedback, and formal assessments. This allows them to capitalize on their strengths for success and address their deficiencies for progress. Not only does this process of self-discovery and progress contribute to an increase in personal effectiveness and pleasure, but it also helps to create a life that is more genuine and satisfying. Individuals are able to manage the complexity of life with greater confidence and resilience when they embrace both their strengths and shortcomings with openness and a dedication to improvement. This eventually results in a more balanced and rewarding existence for the individual.

Recognizing patterns of thoughts and behaviors

The ability to recognize patterns of thinking and behavior is a key component of both self-awareness and the development of one's personality. Individuals are able to gain insights into their fundamental ideas, values, and emotional triggers through the practice of reflective thinking, which enables them to grasp the recurring themes and patterns in their thinking and actions throughout their lives. In order to detect patterns that influence personal well-being, relationships, and general life pleasure, it is essential to have such awareness. These patterns might consist of both constructive and harmful patterns. The significance of understanding these patterns, the means that can be used to do so, and the influence that this awareness has on human development and transformation are all topics that are discussed in this section.

Becoming aware of the fact that a significant portion of our thoughts and actions are habitual is the first step toward comprehending the relevance of detecting patterns of thoughts and behaviors. A person's past experiences, cultural background, and taught behaviors can all contribute to the formation of these patterns, which can become profoundly ingrained. When positive patterns are established, they can result in the development of healthy behaviors, effective coping methods, and good interactions with other people. The opposite of positive patterns is negative patterns, which can lead to self-sabotage, toxic relationships, and an overall feeling of discontent with life. The ability to recognize these patterns gives individuals the ability to strengthen those patterns that are good and change or eliminate those patterns that are not useful, which ultimately results in enhanced mental health and a life that is also more satisfying.

Intentional observation and introspection are necessary steps in the process of detecting patterns in one's thoughts and behaviors. The practice of mindfulness meditation is an reliable method for accomplishing this goal because it teaches people to examine their own thoughts and emotions without passing judgment on them. Individuals can become more tuned in to their internal conversations and emotional responses by frequently practicing mindfulness, which makes it easier to recognize repeating themes and triggers. Mindfulness can be practiced by everyone. In addition to being an effective tool, journaling is a strategy that provides a concrete record of thoughts and activities throughout the course of time. Individuals can benefit from writing about their daily events, thoughts, and feelings since it can assist them in recognizing patterns that they might not perceive in the present. There is a possibility that patterns will form in relation to particular triggers, emotional states, or types of encounters. These patterns can provide useful insights into the manner in which one thinks and behaves automatically.

One of the most important factors in spotting patterns that may be hidden from the individual is the feedback they receive from other people. Outside viewpoints on behaviors and cognitive processes can be provided by friends, family members, and therapists. These relationships can bring to light patterns that the individual may fail to recognize or may choose to ignore. When it comes to recognizing patterns that have an effect on relationships and social interactions, such as communication styles, conflict resolution tactics, and preferences in choosing partnerships, this external input can be especially helpful.

The second step, which comes after the patterns have been recognized, is to comprehend where they came from and what their consequences are. A significant number of thought and behavior patterns can be traced back to early childhood events, cultural influences, or protective mechanisms that were established as a result of previous traumatic experiences. It is possible for individuals to acquire more profound understandings of the reasons for their thoughts and actions by investigating the roots of these patterns, which in turn can facilitate a more sympathetic understanding of themselves. In the context of psychotherapy, professionals can assist individuals in peeling back the layers of their experiences and beliefs, so developing a deeper understanding and facilitating healing. This inquiry can be aided by psychotherapy.

It is equally important to have a solid understanding of the ramifications that these patterns have. Individuals are able to make educated judgments regarding which patterns of thought and behavior to reinforce and which patterns to modify when they are aware of the ways in which particular thinking and behavior patterns influence the outcomes of their lives, the relationships they have, and their emotional well-being. An individual may be able to buffer themselves from immediate discomfort by developing a pattern of avoiding confrontation; nevertheless, this may result in long-term discontent in their relationships. In a similar vein, engaging in a habit of negative self-talk can have an impact on an individual's self-esteem as well as their decision-making processes, which can impede both personal and professional development.

Intention, effort, and frequently help from outside sources are required in order to change unfavorable patterns. Techniques such as cognitive-behavioral therapy (CBT) have the potential to be successful in transforming thought patterns. These techniques assist individuals in challenging negative thoughts and replacing them with more constructive ones. It is possible to make changes in behavior by establishing certain objectives, developing new routines, and actively seeking out settings and relationships that are conducive to positive change. Being patient and having compassion for oneself are essential throughout this process, as altering patterns that have been imprinted in one's mind is difficult and takes time.

The influence of recognizing and changing patterns of thought and behavior is significant and can have a significant impact. More effective emotional regulation, enhanced interpersonal connections, and a more genuine sense of self are all outcomes of this practice. It is common for people who engage in this reflective activity to experience greater levels of life satisfaction, resilience, and a sense of empowerment. They have a greater capacity to deal with the difficulties that life throws at them, to cultivate meaningful relationships with other people, and to pursue objectives that are congruent with their ambitions and beliefs.

In conclusion, one of the most important aspects of both personal development and emotional intelligence is the ability to recognize patterns of thought as well as behavior. Reflection and self-exploration are processes that provide individuals with useful insights into the manner in which they engage with the world and with themselves on a regular basis. Individuals have the ability to greatly improve their mental health, relationships, and the overall quality of life by recognizing these patterns, gaining an awareness of their origins and ramifications, and adopting actions to reinforce positive patterns while changing negative ones. The process of discovering and altering patterns of thinking and behavior is not only difficult but also extremely gratifying. It provides a stepping stone to a life that is more conscious, fulfilled, and empowered.

CHAPTER III

Cultivating Self-Regulation

Strategies for managing and regulating emotions

One of the most important aspects of emotional intelligence is the ability to control as well as manage one's feelings, which has a significant influence on our mental health, the quality of our relationships, and our general quality of life. In spite of the fact that emotions are intrinsically natural and essential, they have the potential to become overwhelming or inappropriate at times, which can result in challenges in both personal and professional settings. It is therefore vital to develop skills for efficiently managing and regulating these emotions in order to navigate the challenges that life presents with fortitude and poise. The purpose of this section is to investigate a variety of techniques for the control of emotions. These techniques include mindfulness, cognitive restructuring, emotional expression, seeking assistance, and physical well-being. Each of these techniques contributes to an all-encompassing approach to emotional health.

In the field of emotion regulation, mindfulness meditation has appeared as a powerful tool that can be utilized very effectively. Focusing one's focus on the here and now while maintaining an attitude of openness and non-judgment is the technique that is being discussed here. It is possible for individuals to achieve greater clarity and perspective by observing their thoughts and feelings without attaching themselves to them. This can result in a reduction in the intensity of unpleasant emotions and an improvement in emotional stability. Mindfulness is a practice that promotes acceptance of emotional events, which in turn reduces the inclination to respond impulsively and makes it possible to formulate answers that are more thoughtful and measured. One's capacity to maintain composure and concentration in the face of emotional problems can be considerably improved via the frequent practice of mindfulness, which can be accomplished through meditation or other mindful activities.

The notion of cognitive restructuring, which has its origins in cognitive-behavioral therapy (CBT), revolves upon the process of recognizing and confronting unpleasant or unreasonable thoughts, which are frequently the fundamental cause of emotional suffering. The realization that our thoughts have an effect on our feelings and actions is the foundation upon which this method is predicated. It is possible for individuals to change their emotional responses if they acquire the ability to detect and modify these thought patterns. Cognitive restructuring is a process that educates people to question the evidence that supports their negative views, to examine alternate interpretations, and to adopt thinking patterns that are more balanced and realistic. Not only does this process assist in the management of initial emotional responses, but it also makes a contribution to the development of long-term emotional resilience.

Expression of emotions is another important method that can be utilized in the management and regulation of emotions. It is possible for individuals to process and make sense of their feelings when they express their emotions in a manner that is healthy and acceptable. This can be accomplished through activities such as talking, writing, or creative activities. When you talk about your feelings with people you trust, such as friends, family members, or therapists, you may find relief, affirmation, and fresh views. In addition, due to the fact that it encourages empathy and mutual support, emotional expression is a vital component in the process of developing closeness and understanding within partnerships. Nevertheless, it is necessary to strike a balance, expressing one's feelings in a manner that is respectful to both oneself and others, without repressing or overindulging one's feelings.

One of the most important aspects of emotional control is the act of seeking help from other people. Support from others can act as a buffer against the negative consequences of stress and emotional upheaval. It is possible to find solace, reassurance, and practical solutions to emotional issues by simply sharing experiences with other people, engaging in meaningful conversations, or getting advice from others. It is essential for one's emotional well-being to have supportive relationships since they not only create a sense of belonging and connection but also enable the expression of emotions. Furthermore, professional support from therapists or counselors can provide expert guidance in the development of effective strategies for emotion regulation, such as solutions that are suited to the specific requirements and circumstances of the individual.

There is a close connection between one's mental health and their physical well-being. The ability to regulate one's mood and emotions can be strongly impacted by factors such as regular physical activity, appropriate sleep, and a balanced diet. There is evidence that physical activity, in particular, can alleviate symptoms of anxiety and depression by triggering the release of endorphins, which are known to improve mood and resilience. Because of the fact that sleep deprivation can make emotional sensitivity and impulsivity worse, getting enough sleep is absolutely necessary for maintaining emotional stability. Furthermore, the decisions that one makes about their nutrition might have an effect on the function of neurotransmitters and, as a result, the regulation of emotions. As a result, ensuring that one's physical health is maintained is a fundamental approach for properly managing one's emotions.

Setting healthy boundaries, engaging in self-compassion practices, and engaging in problem-solving activities are all helpful methods that can be utilized in addition to these strategies for the purpose of controlling and regulating emotions. The act of recognizing and sharing one's limits in relationships and situations is an essential component of setting boundaries, which serves to safeguard one's emotional well-being. Fostering a helpful internal dialogue is an essential component of self-compassion, which means treating oneself with love and understanding during challenging situations. In order to provide a proactive approach to the control of emotions, problem-solving places an emphasis on resolving the problems that are the root causes of emotional pain.

To put these techniques into action, you will need to practice, have patience, and occasionally seek the help of an expert. It is a dynamic process, with different solutions being appropriate for different people because of the diverse circumstances. In order to achieve good emotion regulation, it is essential to maintain an openness to experimenting and acknowledge that the journey toward this goal is both individual and ever-changing.

In conclusion, developing the ability to control and manage one's emotions is a multi-faceted activity that is essential for one's personal development, mental health, and the success of one's relationships. A holistic strategy to navigating the complexities of our emotional landscape can be achieved through the utilization of techniques such as mindfulness, cognitive restructuring, emotional expression, seeking assistance, and preserving physical well-being. Individuals have the ability to enhance their capacity to handle emotional challenges with resilience by incorporating these tactics into their daily lives. This can result in a life that is more emotionally intelligent, balanced, and meaningful. The journey toward emotional regulation is an ongoing process that calls for consistent work and adaptation; yet, the advantages for both one's personal and professional life are significant and far-reaching.

Coping mechanisms for stress and anxiety

In order to successfully traverse the difficulties of modern life, individuals can make use of crucial tools such as coping mechanisms for stress and anxiety. Despite the fact that stress and anxiety are natural reactions to the problems and expectations that we are confronted with, they have the potential to become overpowering and hamper our capacity to perform successfully if they are poorly controlled. Therefore, the development of appropriate coping techniques is absolutely essential for the maintenance of mental health and overall well-being. This section examines a variety of coping mechanisms that might help lessen the impacts of stress and anxiety. These mechanisms include techniques for mindfulness and relaxation, physical activity, cognitive restructuring, time management, social support, and seeking professional assistance.

It is well acknowledged that mindfulness and relaxation practices are among the most effective methods of dealing with stress and anxiety. Through the process of calming the mind and body, practices such as meditation, deep breathing exercises, and progressive muscle relaxation have been demonstrated to be effective in reducing the indications of stress and anxiety. The practice of mindfulness meditation, in particular, enables individuals to concentrate on the here and now, which assists in breaking the cycle of worry and rumination that frequently comes along with anxiety. In a similar vein, activities that involve deep breathing can assist to slow down the heart rate and generate a sensation of calm, while progressive muscular relaxation can help lessen the physical tension that is linked with stress.

One more effective method of dealing with stress and anxiety is to participate in physical activity instead. By participating in regular physical activity, whether it be aerobic exercises such as walking or running, strength training, or yoga, one can considerably enhance their mood and minimize the symptoms of anxiety and depression to a significant degree. Endorphins are chemicals that are discharged in the brain during physical activity. These chemicals have the ability to alleviate pain and boost mood. In addition, engaging in physical activity can act as a distraction, enabling individuals to break free from the vicious loop of negative thoughts that frequently contribute to feelings of worry and stress to increase.

Identifying as well as correcting negative thought patterns that contribute to stress and anxiety is an essential part of cognitive restructuring. Individuals are able to recognize unreasonable or excessive beliefs and replace them with perspectives that are more realistic and balanced through the use of this cognitive-behavioral therapy (CBT) strategy. It is possible for individuals to lessen the intensity of their anxious feelings and experience a greater sense of control over their emotional responses if they make an effort to examine the evidence that supports their worried thoughts, think about alternate outcomes, and concentrate on the positive parts of challenging situations.

It is essential to have effective time management in order to alleviate stress, particularly when the tension is caused by a sensation of being overburdened by duties and deadlines. Individuals can feel more organized and minimize the strain that contributes to stress and anxiety by effective time management tactics such as identifying priorities, breaking things down into smaller parts, and allocating specific time for work and relaxation. These strategies can help individuals feel more in control of their actions. In addition to learning how to say "no" to more duties, one must also learn how to delegate chores wherever it is possible. These are both essential components of time management and stress reduction.

Support from others is an essential component in the process of coping with stress and anxiety. It is possible to experience emotional comfort, practical aid, and a sense of belonging by establishing connections with friends, family members, or support groups. It is possible to ease feelings of isolation and gain new views on difficult situations by sharing worries and experiences with other people who understand. In addition, participating in social activities can work as a distraction and improve one's mood, which is another way in which it can assist in the management of emotional stress and anxiety.

Individuals who discover that their stress and anxiety are having a substantial impact on their day-to-day lives should make it a priority to investigate the possibility of receiving expert assistance. Additionally, therapists and counselors are able to provide support through therapeutic interventions like cognitive behavioral therapy (CBT), offer direction in the development of personalized coping strategies, and, if necessary, recommend medication to assist in the management of symptoms. When individuals are struggling with chronic stress, anxiety disorders, or situations in which self-help measures alone are not sufficient, it can be very advantageous to seek the assistance of other professionals.

A healthy lifestyle, which entails getting enough sleep and eating a balanced food, is also effective in managing stress and anxiety. In addition to these coping techniques, practicing self-compassion, engaging in hobbies and creative pursuits, and keeping a healthy lifestyle are all important. Self-compassion is known as the practice of treating oneself with love and understanding during challenging circumstances. This can help lessen the amount of self-criticism that an individual engages in, which frequently makes anxiety worse. In the same way that a healthy lifestyle supports both physical and mental health, hobbies and artistic activities provide an avenue for expression and a distraction from stressors, those who engage in these activities are more robust to the effects of stress.

To successfully implement these coping methods, you will need to put in work, practice, and be patient. Because coping techniques can vary in their effectiveness based on the person and the scenario, it is essential for individuals to experiment with a variety of tactics and discover the one that works best for them. Moreover, it is of the paramount importance to be aware of the situations in which assistance is required and to not be reluctant to ask assistance when it is required.

In conclusion, it is vital to have coping skills for stress and anxiety in order to navigate the challenges that life presents with resilience and well-being on your shoulder. A holistic approach to managing stress as well as anxiety is provided by these strategies, which include practices such as mindfulness and relaxation, as well as physical activity, cognitive restructuring, time management, social support, and seeking professional assistance. Individuals are able to lessen the burden of stress and anxiety by implementing these coping methods into their day-to-day lives, which ultimately results in improved mental health, increased relationships, and a greater feeling of fulfillment. When individuals have access to the proper resources and assistance, they are able to build a life that is more balanced and serene. The journey toward effective stress and anxiety management is an ongoing one.

Developing impulse control

The development of impulse control is an essential component of emotional intelligence and self-regulation. It enables individuals to make decisions after giving them some thought and to react to situations in a manner that is measured and effective. In order to attain long-term goals or to conform to societal standards and personal values, it is necessary to have the ability to resist current temptations and cravings. This ability is referred to as impulse control. Due to the fact that it has an effect on relationships, productivity, and overall well-being, this capacity is essential for both personal and professional success. The importance of acquiring impulse control, as well as tactics for improving it, as well as the rewards of mastering this essential talent, are discussed in this section.

The significance of being able to regulate one's impulses cannot be emphasized. It is possible that individuals will give in to behaviors that have bad effects if it is not present. These behaviors include excessive spending, excessive eating, substance misuse, and engaging in unsafe activities. The inability to regulate one's impulses can also contribute to challenges in interpersonal relationships, since it can result in improper responses or acts that negatively impact the relationships of others. On the other hand, having excellent impulse control is a contributor to resilience. It enables individuals to negotiate challenges and failures more effectively by focusing on long-term benefits rather than immediate gratification.

Developing the ability to control impulses requires a number of important tactics. The first stage is to increase one's self-awareness, which enables individuals to recognize the circumstances or feelings that cause them to engage in impulsive activities. Self-awareness can be improved by the use of techniques such as mindfulness meditation, which gives individuals the clarity to examine their impulses without instantly acting on them. A pause is created between the stimulus and the response through the usage of this method, which provides individuals with the option to choose how they would like to proceed.

Clearly defining your objectives and gaining a grasp of the motivations behind them is yet another excellent method. When people have a compelling and personal justification for their objectives, they are more motivated to exert self-control and resist impulses in order to accomplish those objectives. Visualizing the long-term rewards of regulating impulses, such as greater health, financial stability, or stronger relationships, can also help to enhance one's dedication to achieving these goals.

There is a direct connection between the practice of delaying pleasure and the improvement of impulse control. A well-known experiment that was conducted in the 1960s by psychologist Walter Mischel and referred to as the "marshmallow test". The purpose of this experiment was to find out whether or not children who were able to wait gratification would have better outcomes in later life. The practice of delaying gratification can be as easy as waiting a few minutes before giving in to a need or putting money away in savings every month before spending it on things that aren't absolutely necessary. The mental muscles that are necessary for impulse control can be strengthened by the use of these techniques over time.

When it comes to impulse control, cognitive restructuring is an extremely important factor. In order to accomplish this, it is necessary to recognize and question the thoughts that are linked to impulsive conduct. Individuals are able to lessen the intensity of their impulses by calling into doubt the veracity of these thoughts and replace them with ones that are more sensible or balanced. As an illustration, rather than thinking, "I have to have this right now," one can think, "I can wait, and the satisfaction of accomplishing my longer-term goal will be greater."

One more practical method to improving one's ability to manage impulses is to create an atmosphere that decreases the number of temptations. For example, if a person has trouble controlling their impulse purchasing, avoiding shopping malls or unsubscribing from marketing emails can help minimize the amount of time they are exposed to temptations. Keeping not healthy snacks out of the house can also be helpful in controlling desires to snack, especially if snacking is a problem in your household.

In order to acquire impulse control, having social support and being accountable to others can be of great assistance. It might be helpful to reinforce one's resolve to achieve one's goals by discussing them with friends or family members who can provide encouragement and comments. In addition, seeking the assistance of a therapist or becoming a member of a support group might provide opportunities to receive advice and encouragement from individuals who are going through similar difficulties.

One last thing to keep in mind when working on impulse control is the need of practicing self-compassion. It is important to treat oneself with kindness and understanding rather than harsh judgment when going through the process of change, which is a process that involves experiencing setbacks. The cultivation of self-compassion fosters a constructive and encouraging internal conversation, which is essential for transformation that is sustained over time.

The benefits of gaining the ability to regulate one's impulses are available in every aspect of life. It allows individuals to concentrate on activities without succumbing to distractions or making hasty conclusions, which is beneficial to their professional lives because it improves productivity and decision-making. Controlling one's impulses makes it easier for individuals to communicate with one another and resolve conflicts in personal relationships. This is because individuals are better able to analyze their replies and the impact of either their words or their actions. The ability to control one's impulses is beneficial to both one's physical and mental health since it encourages the development of healthy habits and reduces the stress and worry that are associated with engaging in impulsive actions.

In conclusion, gaining the ability to regulate one's impulses is a challenging but ultimately gratifying activity that considerably improves the quality of life attained by an individual. Individuals can improve their ability to control impulses by taking steps such as raising their self-awareness, establishing clear goals, engaging in cognitive restructuring, practicing delayed gratification, optimizing their surroundings, finding social support, and practicing self-compassion. Making progress toward improved impulse control is a never-ending process that calls for unwavering commitment and perseverance; nonetheless, the advantages of achieving mastery of this talent are significant and far-reaching.

Practicing mindfulness and meditation

As a potent tool for enhancing well-being, lowering stress, and improving overall quality of life, the practice of mindfulness and meditation is being widely acknowledged as a powerful tool. A better understanding of oneself, emotional regulation, and mental clarity can be achieved through the practice of mindfulness, which is a state of active, open attention to the present moment, and meditation, which is a practice of concentrated focus to develop awareness of oneself and one's surroundings. Together, these two practices offer a pathway to these goals. The core of mindfulness and meditation, as well as their advantages, practical ways to their practice, and the life-altering influence they may have on individuals are all explored in depth throughout this section.

The practices of mindfulness and meditation have their origins in ancient traditions, which date back thousands of years and can be found in a variety of cultural and spiritual contexts. Nevertheless, in the most recent decades, they have been adopted by the western world not just as spiritual practices but also as useful strategies for handling the stressors that are associated with modern living. At their root, mindfulness and meditation are about fostering a heightened state of awareness as well as acceptance of one's thoughts, feelings, body sensations, and the external environment, without judging or reacting immediately to any of these things.

Many advantages can be gained from engaging in mindfulness and meditation practices, and these advantages have been supported by an increasing amount of study in the field of science. Individuals are able to break free from the cycle of negative thought patterns and emotional reactivity that frequently underlies disorders such as stress, anxiety, and depression by the utilization of these techniques, which have been demonstrated to be effective in alleviating these conditions. Mindfulness and meditation are two practices that have been shown to improve cognitive abilities such as attention, concentration, and memory.

These practices educate the mind to concentrate on the here and now and build a sense of mental clarity throughout the practice. Additionally, these practices have been related to enhanced physical health outcomes, like decreased blood pressure, reduced chronic pain, and higher immunological function. This exemplifies the strong connection that exists between the mind and the body.

The practices of mindfulness and meditation are accessible to nearly everyone because they do not require any specialized equipment or a considerable time commitment on the part of the practitioner. Devoting a few minutes of one's time each day to mindfulness meditation, in which the focus is on noticing one's breath, is a straightforward method that can be utilized to get started. When one is seated in a calm environment, they can pay attention to the sensation of the breath entering and leaving the body. They can also pay attention to any ideas, feelings, or physiological sensations that come up, and they can gently return the focus back to the breath if the mind wanders. Through the cultivation of a non-judgmental awareness of the present moment, this practice trains the mind to maintain a state of calm and centering even in the midst of the fluctuations that occur in daily life.

The practice of body scan meditation is another method that can be utilized to improve mindfulness. This method involves focusing one's attention on various parts of the body and observing any sensations, stress, or discomfort that may be present without making any attempt to alter them. By doing so, one might develop a more profound connection with their own body and become aware of the ways in which stress and emotions present themselves physically. Other practices that combine mindfulness concepts include yoga, mindful eating, and walking meditation. These practices encourage individuals to connect fully with the activity at hand and the present moment, which in turn fosters a sense of presence and aliveness.

Beyond the realm of traditional meditation activities, the incorporation of awareness into daily living extends farther. It entails adopting a mindset of mindfulness in order to engage in activities that are commonplace, such as paying close attention to what other people are saying, taking the time to savor a meal, or simply observing the environment with an attitude of openness and curiosity. By adopting this way of thinking about life, routine activities can be transformed into chances for awareness and appreciation, so enhancing the experience of living an ordinary life.

There is a significant and profound impact that can be brought about by practicing mindfulness and meditation. When individuals frequently engage in these practices, they report experiencing a stronger sense of satisfaction and contentment, as well as increased emotional stability, greater resilience in the face of stress, and increased resilience. Individuals are able to examine their sensations without being overpowered by them when they build a space within themselves through the practices of mindfulness and meditation. This results in increased emotional regulation and a reduction in impulsive reactions. A higher level of awareness also encourages feelings of empathy and compassion, not only for oneself but also for other people. This, in turn, contributes to the development of more compassionate relationships and a more compassionate engagement with the world.

Furthermore, persons who engage in the practices of mindfulness and meditation within the context of a spiritual framework may experience spiritual development as a result of their efforts. They encourage a sense of connection to something that is more significant than oneself, and they provide a way to get a knowledge of the nature of the mind and the reality of existence. A person's sense of purpose and meaning in life can be enhanced via the practice of mindfulness and meditation, regardless of the spiritual beliefs that they hold. This can provide a basis for living with intention and feelings of gratitude.

In conclusion, the practice of mindfulness as well as meditation provides a variety of advantages that have the potential to dramatically improve one's mental, emotional, and physical well-being. By engaging in these activities, one can acquire the tools necessary to effectively manage stress, cultivate emotional regulation, and cultivate a profound feeling of presence and awareness. Individuals have the potential to undergo a transition in their relationship with themselves, with other people, and with the world that surrounds them if they incorporate mindfulness and meditation into their everyday lives. Meditation and mindfulness are two practices that offer a road to a life that is more satisfying and well-balanced. The journey of mindfulness and meditation is one of ongoing study and discovery.

CHAPTER IV

Empathy: Understanding Others

Definition and importance of empathy

In human social interactions, empathy is a complicated psychological phenomenon that plays a key role. It influences how individuals connect with one another on a profound and meaningful level, and it plays a part in how people engage with one another. The ability to comprehend and empathize with the emotions of another individual, to perceive the world from their point of view, and to react with compassion and understanding are all included in this concept. As a result of its ability to allow successful communication, establish meaningful relationships, and promote social peace, empathy is frequently regarded as one of the most significant characteristics of emotional intelligence. Through the course of this section, the concept of empathy, its significance in a variety of facets of life, and the influence it has on the well-being of both individuals and groups are investigated.

In its most fundamental form, empathy is comprised of two essential elements: cognitive empathy and emotional empathy. The intellectual capacity to perceive and comprehend the thoughts, beliefs, and feelings of another individual from their point of view is referred to as cognitive empathy. Perspective-taking is another name for that intellectual capacity. Putting oneself in the position of another person, or imagining what they could be experiencing or thinking in a specific circumstance, demands a deliberate effort on the part of the individual.

The ability to physically feel the emotions of another person, almost as if they were contagious, is what is meant by the term "emotional empathy," which contrasts with the concept of "emotional empathy." Individuals are able to connect with one another on an instinctive and visceral level, which helps to build a feeling of shared experience and understanding. This emotional resonance permits individuals to connect with one another.

In every aspect of human existence, from interpersonal interactions to professional settings and even to more general social problems, the significance of empathy cannot be overstated. In the context of human relationships, empathy serves as the adhesive that holds individuals together, allowing them to provide support and understanding to one another as they navigate the difficulty of life. Individuals are able to communicate more effectively, resolve disagreements with compassion, and develop connections that are deeper and more meaningful as a result of this. Through the cultivation of empathy, a culture of trust and respect is fostered, in which every individual is made to feel appreciated and understood, thereby improving the quality and consistency of interactions.

One of the most important skills to have in professional settings is empathy. It acts as the foundation for effective leadership, collaboration, and service to customers. To better motivate and inspire their teams, leaders who demonstrate empathy are better able to comprehend and handle the needs, worries, and goals of their employees. This allows them to better motivate and inspire their teams. Through the promotion of a knowledge of a variety of viewpoints and the cultivation of an inclusive working environment, empathy makes it easier for members of a team to work together productively and cooperatively. Furthermore, in the field of customer service, showing empathy enables professionals to connect with clients or customers on a personal level, which ultimately results in increased levels of satisfaction and loyalty.

It is impossible to overestimate the significance of empathy in society as a whole, which extends beyond the realms of personal and professional matters. The capacity for empathy is the driving force behind prosocial actions, such as assisting those who are in need, fighting for social justice, and working toward the common good. Through this, individuals are able to develop an appreciation for the variety of human experiences, which in turn promotes tolerance, acceptance, and a dedication to equity. Empathy has the ability to bridge the gap between opinions that are in opposition to one another during times of conflict or division, so fostering communication and understanding and paving the way for peaceful settlements.

Because of this, developing and cultivating empathy is an undertaking that is of utmost importance. To interact with the experiences and feelings of others requires attentive attention, an open mind, and a willingness to engage with those experiences and feelings. Teaching children to understand as well as appreciate the feelings of others can be accomplished through the use of educational programs that have an emphasis on social and emotional learning. These programs can play a key part in the development of empathy in children from a young age. Practices such as mindfulness meditation, reading literature that explores many views, and engaging in volunteer work are all examples of activities that can help individuals improve their empathetic understanding and sensitivity.

Empathy has a significant impact on both the well-being of individuals as well as the well-being of groups. Empathy, on a personal level, helps to psychological health and pleasure because it has the ability to strengthen relationships and develop a sense of connection and belonging to those with whom one is interacting. People who are empathic typically report better levels of life satisfaction and lower stress levels. This is because they possess the emotional abilities that are necessary to effectively negotiate the dynamics of interpersonal relationships. Empathy has the capacity to improve society as a whole by fostering social cohesion, lowering levels of prejudice and discrimination, and motivating acts that cater to the requirements of those who are most vulnerable.

Despite the many advantages it offers, the practice of empathy necessitates a sense of equilibrium. On the other hand, excessive emotional empathy can result in emotional burnout or compassion fatigue, which is especially prevalent in professions that involve providing care or in circumstances that involve high emotional exposure. Consequently, it is necessary to acquire the ability to manage one's emotional involvement in order to retain one's mental health while simultaneously being able to provide true support and understanding to other people during this time.

In conclusion, empathy is a fundamental human capability that has far-reaching ramifications for several aspects of life, including personal well-being, relationships, professional achievement, and the advancement of society. It is the capacity to comprehend and empathize with the emotions of other people, so contributing to the development of a world in which people are able to connect with one another through compassion, respect, and mutual understanding. In addition to being a moral necessity, the cultivation of empathy is also a practical necessity because it improves the quality of human interactions and helps to contribute to the development of communities that are more welcoming, supportive, and harmonious. Despite the fact that society is still struggling to find solutions to complex social and global problems, the function of empathy in promoting a sense of common humanity and pushing good change is more vital than it has ever been.

Empathy vs. sympathy

Empathy and sympathy are two basic components of human interaction and emotional reaction, and they are frequently used interchangeably in daily language. On the other hand, they are different notions that each play a distinctive part in the manner in which we interact with other people in times of need, sadness, or joy. In order to cultivate meaningful relationships, provide effective assistance, and successfully navigate the complicated landscape of human emotions, it is essential to have a solid understanding of the distinctions between empathy and sympathy. The definitions of empathy and sympathy, as well as the distinctions between the two, and the significance of each in a variety of settings, are discussed in this section.

Being able to comprehend and identify with the emotions of another individual from their point of view is what we mean when we talk about empathy. Not only does it include recognizing the sentiments that another person is experiencing, but it also involves emotionally connecting with those feelings. This is a profoundly emotional and cognitive process. Empathy enables people to "walk a mile in someone else's shoes," so to speak, which enables them to have a thorough awareness of the emotional condition of the other person experiencing the situation. This shared emotional experience helps to cultivate a true connection and provides a sensation of being understood on a profound level, which can be extremely reassuring and supportive to a person who is going through a tough time.

On the other side, empathy is characterized by the acknowledgment of the emotional struggles of another individual and the provision of comfort, concern, and support, but from a more dispassionate level of view. The act of expressing sympathy does not necessarily involve feeling the emotions that the other person is experiencing. Sympathy, on the other hand, is what motivates an acknowledgment of their suffering and a desire to alleviate it. Words of condolence, gestures of support, and acts of compassion are common ways in which people express their sympathy for another person. Sympathy is a crucial component in demonstrating care and concern, strengthening social relationships, and bringing relief to individuals who are experiencing suffering. Although it does not include sharing the emotional experience, it is nevertheless an essential component.

The degree of emotional involvement and the ability to take into account the viewpoints of others is the primary distinction between empathy and compassion. Being able to empathize with another person demands one to completely submerge themselves in their emotional world and experience their sensations as if they were their own. It is possible that this significant emotional connection will result in a more nuanced knowledge of the circumstances that the person is in, as well as a more profound sense of solidarity and support. Sympathy, on the other hand, is characterized by a certain emotional distance, with the primary focus being on identifying the difficulty and providing support without necessarily engaging in the emotional experience.

Both empathy and compassion are important, but their significance shifts based on the circumstances and the need of the one who is receiving support. Empathy is especially useful in the context of relationships, counseling, and caregiving duties, all of which require an awareness of the emotional intricacies of another person's experience in order to provide effective support. Due to the fact that they transmit a profound level of validation and comprehension, empathic responses have the potential to aid healing, growth, and overall connection. For instance, in a therapeutic environment, the empathy of a counselor can assist clients in experiencing a sense of being seen and understood, which in turn helps to cultivate trust and openness, both of which are necessary for the progression of therapy.

Although it may appear to involve less activities, sympathy is not any less significant. One may not be able to entirely appreciate the perspective of another person due to differences in life circumstances, cultural backgrounds, or personal views; yet, it plays a significant role in expressing solidarity and compassion, particularly in instances where one may not be able to totally comprehend the experience of another. These gaps can be bridged through the expression of sympathy, which provides a type of assistance that acknowledges suffering and demonstrates a want to assist. Through the use of sympathetic gestures, it is possible to convey comfort and reassurance in different situations, so strengthening social bonds and community support.

Both empathy and compassion are essential components of human connection and support when it comes to its practical application. Both empathy and sympathy are able to adapt to a variety of emotional demands and circumstances, with empathy providing a profound and collaborative understanding, and sympathy supplying a reassuring identification. Having said that, it is of the utmost importance to acknowledge the potential difficulties that are involved with each. One example of anything that might contribute to emotional burnout or compassion fatigue is excessive empathy. This is especially true for people who work in caring professions. To guarantee that one can continue to provide empathetic support without becoming overwhelmed, it is necessary to engage in careful self-regulation and to establish boundaries.

On the other hand, having compassion, although its value, can often be interpreted as being superficial or condescending if it is not communicated in a genuine manner or if it fails to acknowledge the extent of the emotional experience that another person is going through. When expressing compassion, it is essential to do it with sincerity and a real desire to offer assistance. This will guarantee that the message is received in the manner that was meant.

When it comes to how we relate to one another and provide support for one another, empathy and compassion are both crucial yet unique components of the relationship. By allowing us to profoundly comprehend and connect with the feelings of other people, empathy enables us to provide tremendous support and solidarity to those around us. Having sympathy allows one to convey care and concern from a more dispassionate stance, while at the same time providing comfort and reassurance to the recipient. Both of these things are quite valuable in terms of developing human relationships, offering support, and constructing communities that are empathetic. By gaining an understanding of the differences between empathy and sympathy, we are able to more effectively respond to the requirements of other people, adapting our help to provide the greatest amount of comfort and assistance that is possible. Through the cultivation of empathy and sympathy, we improve our capacity to negotiate the intricate emotional landscapes of ourselves and others around us. This, in turn, leads to relationships that are more fulfilling and helpful, as well as a world that is more compassionate.

Developing empathy skills

It is a transformative process that increases interpersonal connections, creates deeper understanding, and cultivates compassion in both personal and professional contexts. Empathy skills can be developed via both personal and professional experiences. The capacity to understand and share the emotions of another person is referred to as empathy. Empathy is not only a natural characteristic; rather, it is a talent that can be cultivated and developed over time. In this section, we explore the value of empathy, as well as tactics for its growth and the enormous impact that it can have on relationships, communication, and general well-being.

The realization of the significance of empathy serves as the cornerstone of the process of building empathy abilities. Empathy is more than just the ability to feel another person's emotions; it also involves having a mental and emotional comprehension of the experiences of another person. By doing so, it enables individuals to navigate the world with a heightened sense of compassion and awareness, so removing barriers of misunderstanding and cultivating a culture of love and support. The capacity for empathy builds links within the arena of personal interactions, making it possible for individuals to support one another throughout times of both joy and suffering. Empathy is a professional trait that improves leadership, teamwork, and customer relations, which in turn contributes to a more peaceful and productive work environment.

The practice of active listening is one of the first steps in the process of building empathy abilities. This entails focusing one's whole attention on the words that are being spoken, as opposed to merely listening to the message that is being sent by the speaker. To engage in active listening, the listener must pay great attention to the words, tone, body language, and emotions conveyed by the speaker. This demonstrates that the listener is genuinely interested in and comprehending the information being communicated. Individuals can establish a deep understanding of the ideas and emotions of others by engaging in the practice of active listening, which lays the framework for the development of empathic reactions.

Engaging in activities that stimulate curiosity about other people, particularly those who come from a variety of backgrounds and experiences, is yet another essential method for fostering empathy. In order to satisfy this interest, one must have an open mind and be prepared to investigate and comprehend the distinctive viewpoints, cultures, and life experiences of other others. It is possible to widen one's awareness of the human experience by asking open-ended questions and demonstrating a genuine interest in learning about other people. This can help facilitate the development of a worldview that is more accepting and empathic.

One of the most important aspects of building empathy is regular practice of perspective-taking. The act of actively putting oneself in the position of another person and visualizing their thoughts, feelings, and motives in a specific circumstance is how this is accomplished. An individual's personal prejudices and biases are challenged through the process of perspective-taking, which in turn encourages a more nuanced and sympathetic understanding of the actions and reactions of other people. Due to the fact that it encourages a less judgmental and more empathetic approach, it can be very helpful in settling disagreements and navigating uncomfortable situations.

Regulating one's emotions is another essential component in the process of gaining empathy. Having the ability to control one's own feelings is absolutely necessary in order to respond to other people in a manner that is thoughtful and sympathetic. The ability to recognize one's own emotional triggers and to adopt tactics to maintain composure and objectivity are both essential components of emotional regulation. Individuals who possess this level of self-awareness and control are able to provide support and understanding to others, even when confronted with emotionally charged circumstances.

Increasing one's capacity for empathy can also be accomplished by engaging in reflective practice and soliciting external input. It is possible to gain valuable insights into areas in which one could improve by reflecting on one's interactions with other people and thinking about how one's behavior impacts other people. For the purpose of gaining additional perspectives and direction, it is beneficial to solicit feedback from trustworthy friends, family members, or colleagues regarding one's expressions of empathy. Through this reflective cycle of action, observation, and correction, students are able to continuously learn and improve in their capacity for empathy.

Further development of empathy abilities can be accomplished through a variety of exercises and activities, in addition to the ideas above. Role-playing, for example, gives people the opportunity to experience diverse points of view by putting themselves in the shoes of another person and acting out scenes from their point of view. In addition, the act of reading books and viewing films that investigate a wide range of human experiences can help foster empathy since these activities offer glimpses into the feelings, challenges, and achievements of other people.

Developing empathy abilities has repercussions that extend far beyond the enhancement of one's ability to engage with other people. A greater sense of connection and belonging is fostered through empathy, which in turn improves the emotional well-being of both the person who engages in empathic gestures and the person who receives them. It is possible that this will result in more effective problem-solving and decision-making, as having an awareness of many perspectives will lead to solutions that are more comprehensive and inclusive. Additionally, empathy helps to foster a community that is more empathetic, which in turn encourages acts of kindness, volunteerism, and respect for social justice.

In conclusion, the process of building empathy skills is a journey of continual learning and progress that enhances one's life regardless of whether they are in their personal or professional life. Individuals can improve their capacity to understand and connect with others by participating in activities that promote empathy, practicing active listening, cultivating curiosity, practicing perspective-taking, controlling emotions, engaging in reflective practice, and participating in activities that build empathy. The advantages of possessing these talents are substantial, as they result in the development of stronger relationships, improved communication, and a heightened feeling of compassion and understanding in a world that is becoming increasingly complexity. Not only can empathy help individuals connect with one another, but it also has the potential to influence cultures, thereby making the world a more compassionate and understanding place.

Active listening and perspective-taking exercises

In order to build empathy and good communication abilities, it is essential to have core skills such as active listening and perspective taking. These behaviors not only build stronger relationships with one another, but they also encourage a more profound comprehension and appreciation of the various points of view that exist. To engage in active listening, one must engage in full concentration, comprehend what is being communicated, reply appropriately, and then recall what was said. On the other side, perspective-taking refers to the capacity to put oneself in the position of another individual and to comprehend their emotions, thoughts, and motivations from their point of view. The purpose of this section is to investigate the fundamental purpose of active listening and perspective-taking activities, as well as their significance and the ways in which they can be developed to enhance communication and empathy in both personal and professional contexts.

It is not enough to simply hear the words that are being stated by another person; active listening is a multidimensional ability that goes beyond that. It needs the listener to give their undivided attention, free from any distractions or opinions that they already hold. Attending, comprehending, responding, and remembering are the four essential components that make up the process of active listening or attentive listening. Providing the person who is speaking with your entire attention is the physical act of attending, which is typically exhibited by body language such as making eye contact and nodding occasionally. In order to comprehend something, one must first absorb the information that is being presented and then comprehend the meaning that is behind the words. The response that is offered to the speaker that demonstrates that you are engaged and understood their message is known as responding. This feedback is typically provided in the form of verbal affirmations or summaries of what has been said. Remembering is the capacity to recall and think on the information that was provided, which is an indication that the communication was successful and appreciated.

For the purpose of improving active listening abilities, exercises can be both straightforward and profound. Role-playing exercises, in which participants take turns speaking and listening on a variety of themes, have the potential to be extremely effective. Participants are given the opportunity to practice giving their complete attention, paraphrasing, and asking open-ended questions that stimulate additional conversation through the use of these exercises. Additionally, active listening can be practiced in ordinary interactions by consciously focusing on the speaker, avoiding interruptions, and refraining from developing a response while the other person is still talking. These are all essential components of active listening. An individual's capacity to actively listen can be considerably improved by the use of these activities over time, which can result in interactions that are more meaningful and fruitful.

Understanding the perspectives, feelings, and motives of another individual is an essential component of perspective-taking, which is a skill that complements active listening capabilities. When it comes to empathy, it is an essential component that enables individuals to connect with other people on a more profound level. The act of consciously attempting to see the world through the eyes of another person, which can be difficult but is extremely rewarding, is an example of perspective-taking, which goes beyond empathy. This talent is especially helpful in situations where understanding different points of view is essential, such as when resolving conflicts, managing the dynamics of a team, or any other issue.

In order to cultivate the ability to take perspective, exercises frequently require imaginative engagement and thinking. Individuals are asked to envision a scenario from the perspective of another person, taking into consideration their feelings, thoughts, and motives. This exercise is known as the "Imagine-Other" perspective-taking exercise, and it is an excellent mental exercise. It is possible to improve the effectiveness of this activity by having further conversations on the experience, which will allow for additional exploration and comprehension. Engaging with works of literature, films, or art that provide insight into the lives and experiences of others who are different from oneself is another approach. These kinds of cultural experiences have the potential to introduce fresh perspectives on the world and a deeper comprehension of the complexities of human feelings and experiences.

The incorporation of activities that include active listening and perspective-taking into everyday routines has the potential to have a significant impact on both personal and professional relationships. These talents can lead to more successful teamwork, leadership, and customer service in the workplace by building a setting of mutual respect and understanding. This can be accomplished by implementing these skills. Through the cultivation of stronger links, improved communication, and the capacity to negotiate disputes with compassion and empathy, active listening and perspective-taking are two characteristics that contribute to the development of personal relationships.

To add insult to injury, these abilities have wider-ranging ramifications for the cohesiveness and comprehension of society. The capacity to actively listen to others and to take into account their point of view can help bridge the gap between people and develop a sense of shared humanity in a society that is becoming increasingly split by different points of view and experiences in life. It is possible for individuals to make a contribution to a society that is more understanding and empathic by exercising these talents. Such a society would not merely tolerate diversity but would also respect them.

Therefore, in conclusion, active listening and taking into account the perspectives of others are key skills for effective communication and the development of empathy. Individuals can improve their capacity to connect with others, comprehend a variety of views, and negotiate the intricacies of human interactions with compassion and insight by engaging in focused practice and reflecting on their experiences. Physical activities that concentrate on these abilities can be implemented into daily life, which can result in significant enhancements to one's interactions in both their personal and professional lives. We open ourselves up to a world of deeper understanding and connection when we value and practice active listening and perspective-taking. This highlights the significance of these abilities in the process of constructing a society that is more empathic and cohesive.

CHAPTER V

Mastering Social Skills

Building and maintaining relationships

The cultivation and upkeep of connections are essential components of both personal fulfillment and professional achievement. These interactions, whether they are with members of our family, friends, coworkers, or love partners, serve as the basis of our social life and make a substantial contribution to our emotional and psychological well-being. In order to successfully construct and maintain these connections, one must make an effort, demonstrate comprehension, and demonstrate a dedication to communicating and respecting one another. The purpose of this section is to investigate the fundamental practices and principles that are involved in the process of creating and maintaining good relationships. Particular attention is paid to the significance of communication, trust, empathy, and shared experiences.

Effective communication is the primary factor that contributes to the success of relationships. The ability to communicate one's views, feelings, and requirements in an open and honest manner, while simultaneously listening attentively to the perspectives of others, is essential. Not only does communication involve verbal exchanges, but it also entails non-verbal cues, such as body language and facial emotions, as well as the capacity to understand and respond correctly to these signs. An essential component of good communication is active listening, which entails giving one's undivided attention to the person who is speaking and actively interacting with the message that they are conveying without instantly constructing a response. By demonstrating respect and interest, this degree of attentiveness helps to develop a deeper relationship between the two of you. Resolving misconceptions, preventing confrontations, and strengthening the link between persons can all be accomplished via the practice of active listening and communication that is both clear and compassionate.

Additionally, trust is a fundamental component of healthy relationships. It is constructed over time by behaviors that are constant and reliable, demonstrating integrity, reliability, and a dedication to the connection. by these actions, it is established. In order to establish trust with another individual, it is necessary to have faith in their sincerity and dependability, to have confidence in their capabilities, and to be aware that they can be relied upon. In order to build trust, patience is required because it is a long process that occurs through the accumulation of shared experiences and the reciprocal fulfillment of promises and obligations. After it has been built, trust will make relationships resilient, which will allow them to weather obstacles and disagreements effectively.

Building and maintaining relationships requires a significant amount of empathy, which is defined as the capacity to understand and identify with the emotions of another person. It enables people to connect with one another on a more profound emotional level, which in turn helps to cultivate a sense of mutual understanding and support. Listening to and acknowledging the sentiments of another person is an essential component of empathy, regardless of whether or not one agrees with the other person's point of view. The emotional relationships that are strengthened as a result of this affirmation can be extremely affirming. Individuals are able to negotiate disagreements with delicacy and care when they engage in the practice of empathy. This helps to ensure that even during times of conflict, the underlying respect and affection are preserved.

Relationships can be strengthened via the expression of shared experiences. The creation of memories and the strengthening of bonds can be accomplished by spending quality time together, whether through daily activities, shared hobbies, or exploring new adventures. Laughter, joy, and opportunity for mutual growth are all provided by these events, which contribute to the enrichment of the relationship. Furthermore, overcoming obstacles and moving through the highs and lows of life together can help to strengthen the relationship between the two of you because it exhibits commitment and resilience. A more profound understanding of each other's personalities, interests, and values can also be gained through shared experiences, which can lead to a stronger appreciation and acceptance of one another.

The maintenance of relationships calls for consistent effort and the ability to conform. Relationships evolve in tandem with the development and transformation of persons. It is crucial to maintain open communication about shifting needs, expectations, and boundaries in order to adjust to these changes and ensure that the relationship continues to be healthy and satisfying. Regularly expressing praise and gratitude, enjoying each other's triumphs, and providing support during challenging times are all actions that foster the connection and underline the significance of the relationship.

The ability to resolve conflicts is another trait that is necessary for the maintenance of healthy partnerships. Although disagreements and conflicts are inevitable, the manner in which they are handled can have a considerable effect on the quality of the relationship as well as its longevity. Taking a conflict resolution approach that is characterized by a willingness to understand the perspective of the other party, a dedication to finding a solution that is mutually satisfactory, and an emphasis on keeping the relationship rather than "winning" the dispute can help to prevent long-term damage and even improve the bond between the parties involved.

In conclusion, the act of establishing and sustaining relationships is a dynamic and continuing process that calls for effort, comprehension, and dedication. Strong relationships are built on crucial elements such as effective communication, trust, empathy, and experiences that are shared by both parties. Individuals are able to cultivate deeper connections, learn to negotiate problems more successfully, and take pleasure in the rich, rewarding interactions that lead to a meaningful life when they prioritize these qualities and continuously practice them. It is true that relationships are not devoid of difficulties; yet, if they are approached with caution, patience, and a willingness to invest in them, they have the potential to provide unrivaled support, joy, and friendship.

Effective communication techniques

Successful relationships in personal and professional settings are based on effective communication. It includes the transfer of intentions, feelings, and expectations via a variety of verbal and nonverbal channels in addition to the communication of knowledge. Acquiring proficiency in efficient communication methods is crucial for promoting comprehension, establishing connections, settling disputes, and accomplishing objectives. This section emphasizes the significance and usefulness of several essential components of good communication, such as active listening, succinct and clear expression, emotional intelligence, nonverbal communication, and feedback.

One of the most important aspects of good communication is active listening. It is more than just listening to what is being said; it demands your undivided attention and active participation. Both verbal and nonverbal clues—such as nodding and maintaining eye contact—as well as summarizing or paraphrasing what has been said to show that you comprehend are part of active listening. This tactic promotes an atmosphere that is favorable for candid and open communication by showing respect and interest in the speaker's point of view. In addition to ensuring correct comprehension, active listening fosters rapport and trust—two qualities that are vital to any relationship.

Expressing ideas succinctly and clearly is another essential skill for successful communication. It entails avoiding ambiguity, lowering the possibility of misconceptions, and clearly and understandably expressing thoughts and ideas. This can be especially difficult when explaining complicated concepts or in situations that are complicated. To improve clarity, though, use straightforward language, organize messages rationally, and highlight important elements. Furthermore, adjusting the message to make it most understandable and pertinent to the audience can be accomplished by keeping in mind their background and point of view.

Effective communication is significantly influenced by emotional intelligence. It describes the capacity to identify, comprehend, and control one's own feelings in addition to having the capacity to empathize with those of others. People with high emotional intelligence are able to handle delicate subjects, give constructive criticism, and resolve disputes in a sympathetic and understanding manner. Communicators can improve the efficacy of their interactions by tuning into the emotional undercurrents of a conversation and modifying their tone, phrasing, and style to better suit the requirements and emotional state of their audience.

Body language, facial expressions, as well as tone of voice are examples of nonverbal communication that is highly effective at communicating ideas. These nonverbal clues have a big influence on how the message is interpreted since they can support, contradict, or improve spoken communication. For example, keeping your body language open and initiating eye contact can project sincerity and confidence, while speaking in a friendly tone might demonstrate empathy and approachability. The effectiveness and outcome of interactions can be significantly enhanced by being conscious of, in charge of, and sensitive to one's own non-verbal cues as well as those of others.

As a tool for development, enhancement, and confirmation, feedback is an essential component of good communication. When given carefully and with respect, constructive criticism can promote growth and learning. It entails pointing out both the person's strengths and places for development, making detailed recommendations, and expressing support and belief in their potential to advance. However, proactively seeking out and kindly accepting criticism shows that one is receptive to new ideas and dedicated to both professional and personal development. This mutual feedback-giving and receiving can improve comprehension, promote constructive change, and fortify bonds between people.

Effective communication in real life necessitates flexibility and attentiveness. It is crucial to take into account the communication's objectives, the communicators' relationship, and the interaction's context. Different strategies or a mix of approaches may be needed depending on the circumstances. For instance, whilst precise and succinct communication and non-verbal clues may be prioritized in a presentation, emotional intelligence and active listening may be given more weight in a challenging conversation.

Furthermore, it is a skill that gains from ongoing review and development: effective communication. Over time, one's communication skills can be improved by asking for and receiving criticism from others, reflecting on oneself, and remaining open to new information and changes. In our increasingly international society, it is also crucial to comprehend and navigate cultural differences in communication methods, which calls for sensitivity, respect, and adaptability.

In conclusion, the capacity to communicate effectively is a complex talent that is necessary for success in a variety of spheres of life. It includes nonverbal communication, emotional intelligence, feedback, clear and succinct expression, active listening, and nonverbal communication. Each of these elements adds differently to the quality of interactions. Through the acquisition of these skills and their intelligent, adaptive application, people can enhance their capacity to effectively communicate, establish and sustain connections, settle disputes, and accomplish their goals. Good communication is an essential ability for both professional and personal development because it involves more than just information transfer—it also involves meaningful connections with others.

Conflict resolution strategies

Conflict is inevitable in human relationships, stemming from differences in opinions, beliefs, and values. Whether in personal relationships, workplaces, or broader social contexts, conflicts can either lead to constructive outcomes or exacerbate tensions, depending on how they are managed. Effective conflict resolution strategies are essential for navigating disagreements and fostering a culture of understanding and cooperation. This section explores various strategies for resolving conflicts, emphasizing the importance of communication, empathy, negotiation, and problem-solving in achieving peaceful and productive outcomes.

At the core of conflict resolution is effective communication. Clear, honest, and respectful communication allows all parties involved to express their perspectives, feelings, and needs without fear of judgment or retaliation. Active listening is a critical element of this process, requiring individuals to engage with the speaker fully, understand their message, and acknowledge their emotions. This level of attentiveness demonstrates respect and openness, laying the groundwork for mutual understanding. Furthermore, using "I" statements, such as "I feel" or "I need," instead of accusatory "you" statements, can help convey personal experiences without assigning blame, reducing defensiveness and fostering a more constructive dialogue.

Empathy is significant in resolving conflicts by enabling individuals to see the situation from the other person's perspective. Empathy involves understanding and sharing another's feelings, promoting a deeper appreciation of their experiences and concerns. By empathizing with others, individuals can transcend their own viewpoints, recognize the validity of different perspectives, and identify common ground. This shared understanding can transform conflicts from adversarial stand-offs into opportunities for growth and connection, highlighting the interconnectedness of human experiences.

Negotiation is a direct approach to conflict resolution that involves the parties in conflict coming together to discuss their differences and to seek a mutually acceptable solution. Effective negotiation is based on the principles of fairness, seeking win-win outcomes where possible, and prioritizing the relationship over individual gains. Preparation is key to successful negotiation, requiring a clear understanding of one's own goals, the interests of the other party, and the potential areas for compromise. Maintaining a calm and positive demeanor during negotiation, focusing on interests rather than positions, and being willing to make concessions can facilitate agreement and preserve relationships.

Problem-solving is another vital strategy in conflict resolution, emphasizing collaborative efforts to identify the root causes of the conflict and develop creative solutions. This approach involves brainstorming possible solutions without judgment, evaluating the advantages as well as disadvantages of each option, and selecting the best course of action. Problem-solving encourages a cooperative mindset, shifting the focus from competing against one another to working together against the problem. Involving all parties in the solution ensures that the resolution is sustainable and satisfactory to everyone involved.

Setting clear boundaries and establishing ground rules can also aid in conflict resolution. Boundaries delineate acceptable behavior and ensure that interactions remain respectful and productive. Ground rules might include taking turns to speak, refraining from personal attacks, and keeping discussions focused on the issue at hand. Establishing these guidelines at the beginning of a conflict resolution process can create a safe and structured environment for open dialogue and cooperation.

In addition to these strategies, it is crucial to recognize when external help is needed. When conflicts are deeply entrenched or emotions run high, mediators or professional conflict resolution specialists can provide impartial guidance and facilitate a resolution. These experts can help navigate complex dynamics, ensure that all voices are heard, and assist in developing fair and effective solutions.

Ultimately, the goal of conflict resolution is not merely to end disputes but to strengthen relationships and promote understanding and respect among individuals. Effective conflict resolution recognizes the value of diversity and the potential for growth that arises from addressing and resolving differences. By employing strategies like effective communication, empathy, negotiation, problem- solving, setting boundaries, and seeking external help when necessary, individuals and organizations can transform conflicts into opportunities for learning, innovation, and deeper connections.

In conclusion, conflict resolution is a crucial skill that demands patience, openness, and a commitment to mutual respect and understanding. The strategies discussed in this essay offer a framework for constructively addressing disagreements and finding solutions acceptable to all parties involved. By mastering these techniques and approaching conflicts with a positive and collaborative attitude, individuals can navigate the challenges of human interactions more effectively, fostering a more harmonious and productive environment in all areas of life.

Assertiveness vs. aggressiveness

Assertiveness and aggressiveness are two distinct communication styles that significantly impact interpersonal interactions and the dynamics of personal and professional relationships. Understanding these styles' differences is crucial for effective communication, conflict resolution, and maintaining healthy relationships. While assertiveness is often praised as a positive and constructive approach to expressing one's needs and boundaries, aggressiveness is generally viewed negatively, leading to potential conflict and misunderstanding. This section delves into the definitions, characteristics, and implications of assertiveness and aggressiveness, highlighting the importance of adopting an assertive communication style for fostering respect, understanding, and cooperation in various aspects of life.

Assertiveness is a communication style characterized by confidently and respectfully expressing one's thoughts, feelings, and needs without infringing on the rights of others. It involves clear, direct, and honest communication of one's preferences and boundaries while maintaining a stance of equality in interactions. Assertive individuals are able to stand up for themselves and their rights calmly and positively, seeking win-win solutions that respect both their own needs and those of others. This approach fosters open and honest dialogue, encourages mutual respect, and enhances relationship quality by building trust and understanding.

Assertiveness is grounded in self-awareness, self-respect, and respect for others. It requires a balanced approach that considers both the content of the message and the feelings of all parties involved. Assertive communication addresses issues and expresses needs before they escalate into conflicts. It also involves active listening, empathy, and the ability to negotiate and compromise, demonstrating a commitment to finding mutually satisfactory solutions.

On the other hand, aggressiveness is a communication style marked by asserting one's own needs, rights, or opinions at the expense of others. Aggressive behavior is often confrontational, dominating, and involves the use of intimidation, criticism, or hostility to achieve one's goals. Unlike assertiveness, which seeks to balance one's own needs with those of others, aggressiveness disregards the feelings, needs, and rights of others, leading to potential conflicts and damaging relationships. Aggressive communication can create an atmosphere of fear, resentment, and resistance, undermining trust and cooperation.

The distinction between assertiveness and aggressiveness lies in the manner of expression and the intent behind the communication. Assertiveness aims to express oneself openly and honestly while maintaining respect for others. In contrast, aggressiveness seeks to dominate or control the situation, often resulting in negative emotional responses and breakdowns in communication. Assertive individuals communicate their needs and boundaries without resorting to blame, judgment, or coercion, fostering a constructive and respectful environment.

Developing assertiveness involves understanding one's rights and responsibilities in communication, practicing self-reflection, and learning specific communication skills such as using "I" statements, setting clear boundaries, and expressing oneself directly and respectfully. It also requires building self-confidence and self-esteem, which are foundational for valuing one's own needs and perspectives while respecting those of others.

The benefits of assertive communication are manifold. Assertiveness leads to more effective conflict resolution, allowing for the direct and respectful expression of differing viewpoints and facilitating collaborative problem-solving. It enhances personal and professional relationships by promoting honesty, respect, and mutual understanding. Assertive individuals are more likely to achieve their goals and maintain positive self-esteem, as they effectively advocate for themselves and negotiate for what they need or want.

In contrast, the consequences of aggressive communication can be detrimental. Aggressiveness can alienate others, damage relationships, and escalate conflicts. It can result in feelings of regret, guilt, or low self-esteem in the aggressor and feelings of resentment, anger, or fear in those on the receiving end. Over time, a pattern of aggressive communication can isolate individuals and create a hostile environment, whether at home, in the workplace, or in social settings.

In conclusion, assertiveness and aggressiveness represent two fundamentally different approaches to communication, each with distinct implications for interpersonal dynamics and personal well-being. Assertiveness, characterized by respect, directness, and balance, is a constructive communication style that fosters healthy relationships, effective conflict resolution, and personal growth. Aggressiveness, with its focus on domination and disregard for others' needs, can lead to conflict, damaged relationships, and adverse emotional outcomes. By understanding and practicing assertive communication, individuals can navigate the complexities of interpersonal interactions with confidence and respect, enhancing their relationships and achieving more satisfying and productive outcomes.

CHAPTER VI

Motivation and Goal Setting

Intrinsic vs. extrinsic motivation

Understanding the dynamics of intrinsic versus extrinsic motivation is fundamental to comprehending human behavior and motivation. These two types of motivation are critical in shaping our actions, decisions, and overall approach to life and work. Intrinsic motivation comes from within, which is driven by personal satisfaction and interest in the task itself, whereas external rewards or pressures fuel extrinsic motivation. This section explores the definitions, characteristics, implications, and applications of intrinsic and extrinsic motivation, shedding light on their importance in various contexts, including education, workplace, and personal growth.

The hallmark of intrinsic motivation is acting in a way that fulfills oneself; in other words, doing something because one enjoys it rather than because one is seeking approval from others. When someone pursues an activity because it brings them joy and happiness, that person is acting from an intrinsic motivation. This type of motivation is often associated with high levels of engagement, creativity, and persistence, as the activity is seen as its own reward. Intrinsic motivators include interests, curiosity, challenge, and the pursuit of mastery or personal growth. For example, a person might engage in painting because they enjoy the process of creating art, or they might delve into a research topic because they find the subject fascinating.

Extrinsic motivation, on the other hand, refers to performing an activity to acquire a reward or avoid punishment. External factors, including money, grades, recognition, or avoiding negative consequences drive this type of motivation. While extrinsic motivation can effectively initiate an undesired action, it may not sustain long-term engagement as intrinsic motivation does. For instance, an employee might work overtime to receive a bonus, or a student might study hard to avoid failing a class. Although extrinsic motivation can lead to achievements, it may not foster the same level of personal satisfaction and engagement as intrinsic motivation.

The implications of intrinsic versus extrinsic motivation are profound across various domains. In education, fostering intrinsic motivation among students is linked to deeper learning, creativity, and positive emotional engagement with the material. Educators can encourage intrinsic motivation by creating learning environments that enhance autonomy, competence, and relatedness. When students feel autonomous, they perceive their learning activities as self-chosen and self-endorsed; when they feel competent, they experience mastery and effectiveness in their activities; and when they feel relatedness, they experience a sense of belonging and connection with others.

Understanding and leveraging intrinsic and extrinsic motivation can significantly impact employee satisfaction, productivity, and retention in the workplace. While extrinsic motivators such as bonuses and promotions are common, organizations increasingly recognize the importance of intrinsic motivators. These include providing meaningful work, opportunities for professional development, autonomy, and recognition of employees' contributions. A workplace that nurtures intrinsic motivation can inspire employees to be more innovative, take greater ownership of their work, and commit to the organization's long-term goals.

For one's growth and the achievement of objectives, striking a balance between the intrinsic and extrinsic motivation is also essential. While extrinsic rewards can provide immediate, tangible incentives for actions, intrinsic motivation is often more sustainable, driving long-term commitment and fulfillment. For individuals seeking personal growth, understanding what intrinsically motivates them can lead to more meaningful and satisfying life choices. Pursuing hobbies, careers, and goals that align with one's intrinsic interests and values can enhance well-being and life satisfaction.

Extrinsic and intrinsic motivation do not necessarily have a direct correlation, though. The overjustification effect is a phenomenon wherein extrinsic rewards can sometimes erode intrinsic motivation. When external rewards are introduced for activities that individuals already find intrinsically rewarding, their motivation might shift from internal satisfaction to the external reward, potentially diminishing the initial intrinsic interest. This underscores the need for careful consideration in how and when extrinsic rewards are used, particularly in contexts where fostering intrinsic motivation is the goal.

In conclusion, intrinsic and extrinsic motivation are powerful forces that drive human behavior, each playing distinct roles in how individuals engage with tasks, pursue goals, and find satisfaction in their activities. While intrinsic motivation is driven by personal interest and internal rewards, extrinsic motivation relies on external incentives. Understanding the interplay between these types of motivation is crucial for educators, employers, and individuals alike, as it influences learning, productivity, creativity, and personal fulfillment. By fostering environments that enhance intrinsic motivation and using extrinsic rewards judiciously, it is possible to encourage engagement, achievement, and well-being in various aspects of life.

Setting SMART goals

Setting goals is a fundamental element of personal and professional development. It provides direction, motivation, and a clear focus on achieving specific outcomes. However, not all goals are created equal. The most effective goals are those that are SMART: Specific, Measurable, Achievable, Relevant, and Time-bound. This comprehensive approach to goal setting ensures that objectives are not only clear and reachable but also meaningful and time-sensitive. This section delves into the SMART framework, exploring how each component contributes to creating well-defined goals that enhance the likelihood of success.

The first criterion, Specific, emphasizes the importance of setting clear and unambiguous goals. Instead of broad or vague objectives, specific goals pinpoint precisely what is to be achieved, providing a clear direction for effort and focus. For instance, instead of setting a goal to "lose weight," a more particular goal would be "to lose 10 pounds." This clarity helps to concentrate efforts and resources effectively, making planning and executing the necessary steps toward achievement easier.

Measurable refers to the ability to track progress and assess the outcome of the goal. A goal is measurable when it includes quantifiable criteria that allow for the monitoring of progress. By establishing concrete, measurable indicators of success, individuals can stay motivated and adjust their strategies as needed. For instance, a "increase sales" goal becomes measurable when specified as "increase sales by 20% within the next quarter." Having measurable goals enables individuals to see the tangible results of their efforts, providing motivation and a sense of accomplishment as they progress.

Achievable pertains to the realism of the goal. While goals should be challenging, they must also be attainable given the available resources, skills, and time. Setting achievable goals needs an honest assessment of current capabilities and limitations and the feasibility of overcoming any obstacles. Too ambitious goals may lead to frustration and demotivation, whereas attainable goals foster a sense of efficacy and encourage persistence. For example, setting a goal to run a marathon in a month when one has never run before is less achievable than completing a 5K race within the same timeframe and gradually working up to a marathon.

Relevant ensures the goal aligns with broader objectives, values, and long-term plans. A goal is relevant when it matters to the individual or organization setting it, contributing to broader ambitions and motivations. This alignment ensures that time and effort are invested in truly important and meaningful pursuits, enhancing motivation and commitment. For example, for someone aiming to advance their career in education, a relevant goal would be to pursue additional certification in a specialized teaching method.

Time-bound refers to setting a specific timeframe for achieving the goal. Deadlines create a sense of urgency and help to prioritize tasks and manage time effectively. A time-bound goal establishes a clear endpoint, which can prevent tasks from being indefinitely postponed. For instance, instead of vaguely aiming to write a book, setting a goal to write the first draft by a specific date adds a time constraint that can spur action and progress. Applying the SMART framework transforms the goal-setting process into a strategic and effective practice. To set SMART goals, individuals should start by defining what they want to achieve in specific and concrete terms. Then, they should determine how progress and success will be measured. Assessing the achievability of the goal involves considering the necessary resources, skills, and effort required, ensuring that the goal is challenging yet within reach. The relevance of the goal must be evaluated in the context of larger personal or organizational aspirations, ensuring alignment and meaningful engagement. Finally, establishing a deadline for the goal introduces a timeframe that encourages focus and timely action.

The benefits of setting SMART goals are manifold. This approach clarifies what is to be accomplished and outlines how success will be measured and achieved. It encourages setting realistic and attainable objectives, increases motivation through relevant and meaningful targets, and enhances time management through clear deadlines. SMART goals provide a structured and effective method for goal setting that can lead to greater productivity, achievement, and personal satisfaction.

In conclusion, setting SMART goals is a powerful personal and professional development tool. By ensuring that goals are Specific, Measurable, Achievable, Relevant, and Time-bound, individuals and organizations can create clear, realistic, and meaningful objectives that are more likely to be accomplished. This structured approach to goal setting facilitates success and fosters growth, motivation, and a sense of achievement. Whether in the context of career advancement, personal development, or organizational growth, SMART goals offer a clear path to realizing aspirations and maximizing potential.

Overcoming obstacles and setbacks

Overcoming obstacles and setbacks is integral to the human experience, defining our resilience, character, and ultimately, our achievements. Life's journey is seldom a straight path; it is fraught with challenges that test our resolve, patience, and adaptability. These personal, professional, or social hurdles can initially seem impossible. However, they also present opportunities for growth, learning, and profound self-discovery. This section explores strategies for overcoming obstacles and setbacks, emphasizing the importance of resilience, perspective, support systems, and learning from failure.

Resilience stands at the forefront of overcoming challenges. The psychological strength enables individuals to bounce back from adversities, emerging stronger and more resourceful. Developing resilience involves cultivating a positive mindset, focusing on solutions rather than problems, and maintaining a steadfast belief in one's abilities. It also entails accepting that setbacks are a natural part of progress, not failure indicators. Resilient individuals view obstacles as temporary and surmountable, an attitude that fuels persistence and determination.

Maintaining perspective is crucial when faced with setbacks. It's easy to be overwhelmed by the immediacy of a problem, losing sight of the bigger picture. To gain perspective, individuals can practice mindfulness, which encourages living in the present and acknowledging one's feelings without judgment. This can help mitigate the stress and anxiety that often accompany setbacks. Additionally, reframing challenges as opportunities for growth can shift one's focus from victimhood to empowerment. By asking, "What can I learn from this?" rather than lamenting over misfortune, individuals can find value in adversity and motivate themselves to move forward.

A strong support system is invaluable in overcoming obstacles. Friends, family, mentors, or professional counselors can offer emotional support, practical advice, and alternative perspectives. Sharing one's struggles with trusted individuals can lessen the burden, provide relief, and open up avenues for assistance that one might not have considered. Support networks also offer encouragement and validation, reminding individuals of their strengths and past successes, which can be especially uplifting during times of doubt and uncertainty.

Learning from failure is an essential part of overcoming setbacks. Every obstacle presents a lesson, whether it's about personal limitations, flawed strategies, or external factors. Reflecting on these lessons allows for personal and professional development. It involves analyzing what went wrong, what could have been done differently, and how to improve in the future. This process transforms setbacks into stepping stones toward success, embedding valuable insights and strategies that enhance one's approach to future challenges.

Setting realistic goals as well as breaking them down into manageable steps can also facilitate overcoming obstacles. Clear, achievable objectives provide direction and a sense of purpose, making daunting tasks seem more approachable. Celebrating small victories along the way fosters motivation and a positive outlook, reinforcing the belief that progress is being made, no matter how incremental it may seem.

Embracing flexibility and adaptability is another strategy for navigating setbacks. Adjusting one's approach in response to obstacles is a hallmark of resilience and creativity. It requires an openness to change and the willingness to experiment with new strategies. Flexibility enables individuals to pivot in the face of unforeseen challenges, exploring alternative paths to their goals.

Finally, practicing self-care and maintaining physical and mental health are foundational to overcoming obstacles. Stress as well as anxiety can take a toll on one's well-being, impairing the ability to think clearly and act decisively. Regular exercise, healthy eating, adequate sleep, and relaxation techniques such as meditation can bolster physical and mental resilience, providing the energy and clarity needed to tackle challenges.

In conclusion, overcoming obstacles and setbacks is a multifaceted process that requires resilience, perspective, support, learning from failure, goal-setting, flexibility, and self-care. While challenges are inevitable, our responses to them define our path to growth and fulfillment. By embracing these strategies, individuals can navigate life's hurdles with grace and determination, turning obstacles into personal and professional development opportunities. The journey through adversity is not only about reaching the destination but also about the wisdom gained, the strengths discovered, and the character forged along the way.

Finding purpose and passion

Finding purpose and passion in life is a quest that many embark upon, seeking a sense of fulfillment and direction that transcends the everyday routines and challenges. This pursuit is profoundly personal and varies significantly from one individual to another, yet it is universally tied to a sense of meaning, happiness, and well-being. Discovering one's purpose and passion involves introspection, exploration, and a willingness to embrace change and challenges. This section delves into the journey of finding purpose and passion, outlining strategies for uncovering these driving forces and their impact on personal and professional lives.

Purpose can be understood as a sense of overarching direction or a call to contribute to something greater than oneself. It is often associated with long-term goals and a vision for one's life that aligns with personal values and beliefs. On the other hand, passion is the intense enthusiasm or excitement for activities, subjects, or pursuits that deeply engage and energize an individual. While purpose gives life a sense of meaning and direction, passion fills it with joy, curiosity, and a sense of fulfillment.

The journey to finding purpose and passion begins with self-reflection. This involves considering what truly matters to an individual, what brings them joy, and what they feel naturally drawn to. Questions such as "What activities make me lose track of time?" or "What issues do I feel strongly about?" can help unearth underlying passions and potential purposes. Reflecting on moments of deep satisfaction or achievement can also provide clues to what one finds meaningful and fulfilling.

Exploration and experimentation are key to discovering passions that may not be immediately apparent. Trying new activities, learning new skills, and stepping out of one's comfort zone can reveal hidden interests and talents. This exploration process is not just about identifying what one loves doing but also about understanding what one cares deeply about. It may involve volunteering, traveling, pursuing hobbies, or engaging with different communities and cultures. Through exploration, individuals can gather experiences that shape their understanding of themselves and the world, helping to refine their sense of purpose and passion.

Connecting with others who share same interests or embody a sense of purpose and passion can also be incredibly insightful. Such connections can inspire, challenge, and motivate individuals to pursue their own paths more vigorously. Networking, mentorship, and community engagement can provide support, guidance, and new perspectives that enrich the journey toward finding purpose and passion.

Setting goals as well as creating a vision for the future are practical steps that can help translate purpose and passion into actionable plans. This involves considering how one's passions can be integrated into daily life or career paths and setting short-term and long-term goals that reflect one's purpose and values. Writing a personal mission statement can also be a powerful exercise in defining one's purpose and outlining how it can be pursued in various aspects of life.

It's essential to recognize that finding purpose and passion is not a one-time event but a continuous process of growth and discovery. Passions can evolve, and purposes can expand as individuals learn, experience, and change over time. Therefore, maintaining an open mind, practicing resilience in the face of setbacks, and being willing to reassess and adjust one's direction are crucial aspects of this lifelong journey.

The impact of finding purpose and passion extends far beyond personal fulfillment. Individuals who have a clear sense of purpose and engage in activities they are passionate about tend to exhibit higher levels of creativity, motivation, and resilience. They are more likely to take initiative, overcome obstacles, and achieve their goals. Furthermore, living with purpose and passion can improve mental and physical health, enhance relationships, and contribute to a sense of connectedness and contribution to the broader community.

In professional contexts, aligning one's work with personal purpose and passion can lead to greater job satisfaction, productivity, and success. It can inspire innovation, foster engagement, and drive excellence, benefiting both the individual and the organization. However, it's also important to recognize that purpose and passion can be pursued outside of work, in hobbies, volunteer activities, or family life, contributing to a well-rounded and fulfilling life.

In conclusion, finding purpose and passion is an enriching journey that enhances the quality of life, drives personal growth, and contributes to a sense of fulfillment and well-being. Through self-reflection, exploration, goal-setting, and continuous learning, individuals can discover and pursue what truly matters to them. While the path to finding purpose and passion may be fraught with challenges and uncertainties, it is also filled with opportunities for joy, discovery, and meaningful contribution. Embracing this journey with an open heart and mind can transform individual lives and the world around us, as individuals who live with purpose and passion inspire and uplift those around them.

CHAPTER VII

Emotional Intelligence in Leadership

The role of Emotional Intelligence in leadership

The significance of emotional intelligence (EI) in leadership is becoming more largely acknowledged as an essential component of a leader's performance, adaptability, and success in a variety of industries. Leadership techniques are greatly impacted by emotional intelligence, which is the capacity to identify, regulate, and affect both one's own emotions as well as those of others. It enhances decision-making, team dynamics, conflict resolution, and overall organizational climate. This section explores the multifaceted role of EI in leadership, highlighting how it contributes to developing empathetic, adaptable, and influential leaders capable of navigating the complexities of the modern workplace.

At the heart of Emotional Intelligence is self-awareness, a critical component for any leader. Self-aware leaders have a profound understanding of their emotions, strengths, weaknesses, and values. They know how their feelings can affect their thoughts, decisions, and interactions with others. This awareness is crucial for self-regulation, enabling leaders to control impulses, manage stress effectively, and maintain professionalism in challenging situations. Leaders high in EI can thus navigate the highs and lows of leadership with composure, inspiring confidence and stability within their teams.

Empathy, or the capacity to feel what others are feeling, is another essential component of emotional intelligence

(EI) in leadership. Leaders who have empathy are able to establish robust connections with their team members by acknowledging their unique needs, apprehensions, and driving forces. This understanding fosters a supportive and inclusive work environment, encouraging open communication and collaboration. By valuing and addressing the emotional well-being of their teams, empathetic leaders enhance employee satisfaction, loyalty, and performance. Empathy also aids in conflict resolution, as leaders can navigate disputes with a balanced understanding of all perspectives involved, leading to more equitable and effective solutions.

Social skills, a component of EI, are indispensable for effective leadership. These skills encompass communication, conflict management, persuasion, and team building. Leaders with strong social skills can articulate their vision compellingly, motivate their teams, and foster a collaborative culture. They are adept at managing relationships and networks, negotiating conflicts without alienating parties, and creating a sense of community and shared purpose. These abilities are essential for leading diverse teams, driving change, and achieving organizational goals.

Emotional Intelligence is significant in decision-making. Leaders often face complex decisions involving uncertainty and competing interests. High EI enables leaders to process emotional information and consider the human aspect of their decisions. It allows for a balanced consideration of logical and emotional inputs, leading to decisions that are effective, resonate with the team, and align with organizational values. This emotionally informed decision-making process can enhance trust and respect among team members, as they feel their perspectives and feelings are valued.

Furthermore, EI contributes to resilience and adaptability in leadership. The contemporary business environment is characterized by the rapid change and uncertainty. Leaders high in EI can manage their emotions during crises, remain flexible in the face of change, and guide their teams through transitions with optimism and clarity. This resilience inspires confidence and adaptability within teams, essential qualities for navigating disruptions and emerging stronger on the other side.

The development and enhancement of EI in leaders is achievable through continuous learning and practice. Self-reflection, feedback from peers and mentors, coaching, and targeted training can help leaders improve their emotional intelligence skills. By committing to personal growth in this area, leaders can significantly impact their effectiveness and the success of their organizations.

In conclusion, Emotional Intelligence is a critical determinant of successful leadership. It encompasses self-awareness, empathy, social skills, effective decision-making, and resilience, all of which are essential for leading effectively in today's complex and dynamic work environment. Leaders who cultivate and demonstrate high levels of EI can build stronger teams, foster a positive organizational culture, and achieve superior outcomes. As the corporate landscape continues to evolve, the value of Emotional Intelligence in leadership will only continue to grow, highlighting the need for current and aspiring leaders to develop this indispensable skill set.

Leading with empathy and authenticity

Leading with empathy and authenticity has emerged as a paradigm shift in the realm of leadership, moving away from traditional authoritarian models towards a more human-centered approach. This shift acknowledges the complex, multifaceted nature of human motivations and the value of genuine connections in the workplace.

Empathy, which is the ability to understand and to share the feelings of another, combined with authenticity, being true to one's own personality or spirit, creates a powerful leadership style that fosters trust, respect, and loyalty. This section explores the significance of leading with empathy and authenticity, detailing how these qualities enhance leadership effectiveness, promote a positive organizational culture, and drive performance.

Empathy in leadership involves actively listening to and understanding team members' perspectives, needs, and concerns. It requires leaders to step into their employees' shoes, appreciate their unique situations, and respond with sensitivity and support. This empathetic approach builds a strong rapport between leaders and their teams, creating an environment where individuals feel valued and understood. Employees who believe their leaders genuinely care about their well-being are more engaged, motivated, and committed to their work and the organization's goals. Empathy also aids in conflict resolution, as empathetic leaders can navigate disputes with a balanced understanding of all perspectives involved, leading to more equitable and effective solutions.

Authenticity in leadership, on the other hand, involves being transparent, honest, and consistent in one's actions and decisions. Authentic leaders do not wear a façade; they lead by example, aligning their words with their actions and staying true to their values and beliefs. This authenticity fosters trust and respect within the team, as employees are more likely to follow a genuine and moral leader. Moreover, authentic leaders create a culture of openness and continuous learning by demonstrating vulnerability and admitting to mistakes. This humanizes the leader, making them more relatable, and encourages a similar level of honesty and self-reflection among team members.

The combination of empathy and authenticity in leadership has profound implications for organizational culture. It cultivates an atmosphere of psychological safety, where employees feel secure expressing their ideas, taking risks, and admitting failures without fear of retribution. This open, supportive environment is conducive to innovation, as individuals are encouraged to think creatively and explore new possibilities. Furthermore, leading with empathy and authenticity promotes diversity and inclusion by valuing and respecting the unique contributions of each team member, despite of their background or position.

In terms of performance, an empathetic and authentic leadership style can lead to superior outcomes. Teams led by empathetic and authentic leaders are often more cohesive, collaborative, and productive. The strong bonds of trust and respect that develop in such teams enhance communication and coordination, making it easier to achieve common goals. Additionally, when leaders recognize and address their team members' individual needs and motivations, they can tailor their leadership approach to maximize engagement and performance.

Developing empathy and authenticity as leadership qualities requires a commitment to personal growth and self-awareness. Leaders can enhance their empathetic abilities by practicing active listening, seeking to comprehend before being understood, and regularly soliciting and acting on feedback from their teams. To cultivate authenticity, leaders should engage in self-reflection, clarify their values and principles, and ensure that their actions consistently reflect these values. Moreover, leaders can benefit from mentoring relationships and professional development opportunities focusing on emotional intelligence and authentic leadership practices.

However, leading with empathy and authenticity also presents challenges. Leaders must balance compassion with accountability, ensuring empathy does not compromise performance standards or enable counterproductive behaviors. Similarly, while authenticity demands honesty, leaders must distinguish between transparency and discretion, particularly in sensitive situations. Despite these challenges, the benefits of leading with empathy and authenticity far outweigh the potential drawbacks, offering a more sustainable and human-centered approach to leadership.

In conclusion, leading with empathy and authenticity represents a powerful and effective leadership style that resonates with the values and needs of today's workforce. By fostering genuine connections, understanding, and trust, empathetic and authentic leaders can create positive organizational cultures that encourage engagement, innovation, and performance. As the business landscape continues to evolve, emphasizing the human aspects of leadership will become increasingly important for attracting, retaining, and motivating talent. Leaders who embrace and develop these qualities will be well-equipped to navigate the intricacies of the modern workplace, driving success for their teams and organizations.

Creating a positive work culture

A positive work culture fosters a productive, innovative, and satisfying workplace environment. A positive culture enhances employee well-being, attracts and retains top talent, and drives organizational success. It is characterized by values such as respect, integrity, openness, and inclusivity, and is manifested through practices that prioritize employee engagement, collaboration, and development. This section explores the critical elements of creating a positive work culture:

leadership, communication, recognition, professional development, work-life balance, diversity, and inclusion.

Leadership is pivotal in shaping work culture. Leaders set the tone for the organizational climate by modeling the values and behaviors they wish to see throughout the workplace. Effective leaders are not just managers of tasks but also visionaries who inspire trust, motivate performance, and foster a sense of purpose among employees. They practice empathy, listen actively, and show genuine interest in the well-being of their team members. Integrity and transparency in leadership are essential for creating a pleasant work environment, and they can help leaders foster a culture of respect and trust.

Communication is another cornerstone of a positive work culture. Open and honest communication creates a foundation for mutual understanding and cooperation. Organizations should encourage a culture where feedback is freely exchanged, ideas are valued, and employees feel heard. This can be obtained through regular team meetings, one-on-one check-ins, and accessible communication channels that facilitate dialogue across all levels of the organization. Clear communication about company goals, changes, and expectations also helps employees feel informed and engaged, contributing to a sense of inclusion and alignment with the organization's mission.

Recognition and appreciation are powerful tools for building a positive work culture. Acknowledging employees' efforts and achievements reinforces their value to the organization, boosts morale, and motivates continued excellence. Recognition can take many forms, from public acknowledgment in meetings to personalized notes of thanks, awards, or performance-based bonuses. Celebrating both individual and team successes fosters a culture of appreciation and encourages a collective commitment to the organization's goals.

Professional development is critical for employee satisfaction and organizational growth. A positive work culture supports continuous learning and career advancement, offering opportunities for training, mentorship, and skill-building. By investing in employees' professional development, organizations demonstrate a commitment to their team members' futures, enhancing loyalty and motivation. Furthermore, empowering employees with the skills and knowledge they need to succeed facilitates innovation and adaptability, critical components of a thriving organizational culture.

Work-life balance is increasingly recognized as an essential aspect of a positive work culture. Organizations that respect and promote work-life balance acknowledge the importance of personal time for rest, recreation, and family. This can be supported through flexible work arrangements, like remote work options, flexible schedules, and policies discouraging overwork. Cultivating an environment where employees feel their personal lives are valued contributes to overall well-being, reduces burnout, and enhances job satisfaction.

Diversity as well as inclusion are integral to creating a positive work culture. A diverse and inclusive workplace values and leverages all employees' unique backgrounds, perspectives, and talents. This requires proactive measures to ensure equal opportunities, address biases, and create an environment where everyone feels respected and included. Celebrating diversity and fostering an inclusive culture not only enriches the workplace experience for employees but also drives creativity, innovation, and better decision-making by incorporating a wide range of viewpoints.

In conclusion, building a positive work culture is a multifaceted endeavor that requires intentional effort from leadership and active participation from all employees. It is built on a foundation of respect, trust, and shared values, and is characterized by practices that promote open communication, recognition, professional development, work-life balance, and diversity and inclusion. By prioritizing these elements, organizations can cultivate a work environment that attracts as well as retains top talent, fosters employee well-being, and drives organizational success. A positive work culture is not just beneficial for employees; it is a strategic asset that enhances competitiveness, adaptability, and long- term sustainability in an ever-changing business landscape.

Case studies of emotionally intelligent leaders

Emotionally intelligent leaders can navigate complex interpersonal dynamics, inspire teams, and drive organizational success with compassion and understanding. In leadership, emotional intelligence (EI) encompasses self-awareness, self-regulation, motivation, empathy, and social skills. This section explores case studies of leaders who have exemplified these components of EI, demonstrating the profound impact emotionally intelligent leadership can have on an organization's culture, employee engagement, and overall performance.

One notable example of emotionally intelligent leadership is that of Satya Nadella, CEO of Microsoft. Taking the helm in 2014, Nadella embarked on a mission to transform Microsoft's culture from one known for its competitiveness and internal rivalry to one focused on collaboration, innovation, and empathy. Nadella emphasized the importance of empathy in product development and understanding his team's needs and strengths. Under his leadership, Microsoft has seen a resurgence in innovation, employee morale, and market value. Nadella's approach to leadership underscores the value of empathy and the belief that understanding and addressing the needs of employees and customers alike can drive growth and success.

Another example of an emotionally intelligent leader is Indra Nooyi, the former CEO of PepsiCo. Nooyi was known for her deep commitment to her employees' well-being and professional development. She believed in the power of personal connection, often writing letters to the parents of her senior executives to thank them for the values they instilled in their children, which she believed contributed to their success at PepsiCo. This gesture demonstrated Nooyi's appreciation for the holistic development of her team members and highlighted her understanding of the importance of family and upbringing in shaping individuals. Her leadership style fostered a sense of loyalty, respect, and motivation among PepsiCo's employees, contributing to the company's enduring success.

Mary Barra, CEO of General Motors (GM), exemplifies the importance of self-awareness and self-regulation in emotionally intelligent leadership. Barra took the lead at GM during a tumultuous time, facing significant challenges, including a major safety recall. Her response to the crisis demonstrated a commitment to transparency and accountability and a profound sense of empathy for the victims and their families. Barra's ability to manage her emotions under pressure, communicate openly about the company's mistakes, and take decisive action to address the issues helped restore trust in GM's leadership and brand. Her leadership highlights how self-regulation and a clear, empathetic communication strategy can steer an organization through crisis and rebuild its reputation.

Sheryl Sandberg, COO of Facebook, has been a vocal advocate for emotional intelligence in the workplace, particularly regarding empathy and social skills. Following the sudden death of her husband, Sandberg wrote about her experience of grief and the importance of support and empathy from colleagues during difficult times. She has encouraged a work culture where personal struggles are acknowledged and supported, advocating for policies that help employees through challenging periods. Sandberg's leadership and advocacy work demonstrates how personal experiences can inform a leader's approach to empathy and social support within the organization, fostering a culture of understanding and compassion.

Finally, the leadership of Tony Hsieh, the late CEO of Zappos, provides a compelling case study in the motivation and social skills aspects of emotional intelligence. Hsieh was renowned for his focus on company culture and employee happiness, believing that a positive work environment was crucial to business success. Under his leadership, Zappos became known for its exceptional customer service, which directly reflected its internal culture. Hsieh's vision involved creating a community of mutual respect, open communication, and shared purpose, demonstrating how a leader's motivation to build a positive organizational culture can result in outstanding performance and innovation.

These case studies of emotionally intelligent leaders illustrate the transformative power of EI in leadership. Leaders like Satya Nadella, Indra Nooyi, Mary Barra, Sheryl Sandberg, and Tony Hsieh demonstrate that leadership is not just about strategic vision or operational excellence; it's equally about understanding and managing emotions—both one's own and those of others. Their successes underscore the importance of empathy, self-awareness, motivation, and social skills in building resilient, innovative, and cohesive teams and organizations.

In conclusion, emotionally intelligent leadership is a critical determinant of organizational success. The leaders discussed in this essay exemplify how emotional intelligence can shape company culture, drive employee engagement, navigate crises, and lead with compassion and authenticity. Their leadership journeys provide valuable lessons for current and aspiring leaders on the importance of cultivating emotional intelligence to inspire, motivate, and lead more effectively. As the business landscape evolves, the demand for emotionally intelligent leadership will undoubtedly increase, highlighting the need for leaders to develop and harness these essential skills.

CHAPTER VIII

EQ in Personal Growth

Applying Emotional Intelligence to personal development

Emotional Intelligence (EI) is a potent tool for navigating the complexities of interpersonal relationships and fostering personal growth and development. Applying EI to personal development involves harnessing the ability to understand as well as manage one's own emotions, as well as to identify and influence the emotions of others. This procedure can lead to increased self-awareness, improved self-regulation, enhanced motivation, more profound empathy, and refined social skills. This section explores how each component of EI contributes to personal development, offering insights into how individuals can cultivate these skills to achieve greater emotional well-being, fulfillment, and success in various aspects of life.

Self-awareness, the cornerstone of EI, is the ability to recognize and understand one's own emotions, strengths, weaknesses, values, and drivers. Developing self-awareness involves regularly reflecting on one's feelings, reactions, and behaviors, seeking to understand the underlying causes and patterns. This introspective practice allows individuals to gain a deeper understanding of themselves, facilitating personal growth by highlighting areas for improvement and strengths to build upon. Increased self-awareness also enables individuals to make more educated decisions that align with their values and goals, leading to a more authentic as well as fulfilling life.

Self-regulation, another critical aspect of EI, involves effectively managing one's emotions and impulses. By applying self-regulation to personal development, individuals can learn to control negative emotions including anger, frustration, or anxiety, preventing them from derailing their goals or harming their relationships. Techniques such as mindfulness, deep breathing, and cognitive restructuring can help individuals regulate their emotional responses, fostering resilience in the face of challenges and setbacks. Improved self-regulation also enhances an individual's ability to stay focused, maintain motivation, and pursue their goals with discipline and persistence.

Motivation, driven by understanding one's emotions, is essential for setting and achieving personal and professional objectives. Emotionally intelligent individuals can channel their emotions into positive motivation, using their passion and enthusiasm to fuel their efforts. They set challenging yet achievable goals, remain optimistic in the face of adversity, and derive satisfaction from pursuing excellence. By leveraging their intrinsic motivation, individuals can maintain a high level of engagement and commitment to their personal development, continuously striving to learn, grow, and achieve success.

Empathy, the capacity to understand and to share the feelings of others, is also beneficial for personal development. Individuals can improve their relationships, enhance their communication skills, and foster a deeper connection with those around them by cultivating empathy. Empathy allows individuals to appreciate different perspectives, promoting tolerance and compassion. It also enhances emotional support and understanding within relationships, contributing to a supportive social network that is invaluable for personal growth and well-being.

Social skills, encompassing effective communication, conflict resolution, and teamwork, are enhanced through the application of EI. Developing strong social skills enables individuals to build positive relationships, navigate social complexities, and influence others effectively. Individuals can improve their interactions and collaboration by practicing active listening, assertive communication, and constructive feedback. These skills are necessary for personal and professional success, as they facilitate networking, leadership opportunities, and the capacity to work effectively in different teams.

Applying EI to personal development is a dynamic and ongoing process. It involves continuous learning, self-reflection, and practice. Individuals can cultivate their EI by seeking feedback from others, engaging in emotional intelligence training programs, and applying EI principles in their daily interactions and decisions. Challenges and setbacks provide opportunities to practice and strengthen EI skills, contributing to personal growth and emotional resilience.

The benefits of applying EI to personal development are manifold. Individuals with high EI enjoy improved mental and emotional well-being, as they can navigate their emotions effectively and maintain a positive outlook. They experience more satisfying and enduring personal and professional relationships due to their empathy and social skills. Additionally, emotionally intelligent individuals are better equipped to achieve their goals, as they can harness their motivation, navigate challenges with resilience, and collaborate effectively with others.

In conclusion, applying Emotional Intelligence to personal development offers a comprehensive framework for enhancing self-awareness, self-regulation, motivation, empathy, and social skills. These components of EI are instrumental in fostering personal growth, emotional well-being, and success in various life domains. Individuals can embark on a voyage of continuous self-improvement by intentionally cultivating EI, leading to a more fulfilling, resilient, and connected life. Applying EI principles to personal development benefits the individual and has a positive impact on their relationships and communities, highlighting the transformative power of emotional intelligence.

Cultivating resilience in the face of challenges

Cultivating resilience in the face of challenges is a vital skill for navigating the complexities and uncertainties of life. Resilience, the ability to bounce back from setbacks, adapt to change, and keep going in the face of adversity, is not an innate trait but a capacity that can be developed and strengthened over time. This section explores the concept of resilience, strategies for building it, and the profound impact resilience can have on individuals' ability to overcome difficulties and thrive despite them.

Resilience begins with recognizing that challenges and setbacks are an inevitable part of life. Rather than perceiving difficulties as insurmountable obstacles, resilient individuals view them as opportunities for learning and development. This mindset, often called a growth mindset, is fundamental to resilience. It fosters adaptability and encourages individuals to approach problems with curiosity and openness, seeking solutions and learning from the experience, rather than being overwhelmed by the perception of failure.

A key strategy for cultivating resilience is developing a strong support network. Relationships with family, friends, colleagues, and mentors provide emotional support, practical assistance, and also a sense of belonging that can buffer against the stress of challenges. These connections offer different perspectives, advice, and encouragement, reminding individuals that they are not alone in their struggles. Actively maintaining and nurturing these relationships ensures a reliable support system is in place when difficulties arise.

Self-care is another critical aspect of building resilience. Physical and emotional well-being are interlinked, and taking care of one's physical health through balanced diet, regular exercise, and sufficient sleep can improve emotional resilience. Exercise, in particular, is known to reduce symptoms of anxiety and depression, improve mood, and increase energy levels, all of which contribute to a greater capacity to handle stress. Similarly, practices such as mindfulness, meditation, and relaxation techniques can help manage stress and emotions, fostering a calm and centered approach to challenges.

Setting realistic goals and taking decisive action is essential for resilience. When faced with a challenge, resilient individuals break down the problem into manageable parts, set achievable goals for addressing each part, and take concrete steps toward solving the problem. This proactive approach empowers individuals, giving them a sense of control and purpose that can mitigate feelings of helplessness and despair.

Another critical component of resilience is maintaining a positive outlook. This does not mean ignoring reality or glossing over problems but rather focusing on what can be controlled and finding reasons to be hopeful. Practicing gratitude, celebrating small victories, and reminding oneself of past successes can reinforce a positive attitude. Optimism, a belief in a positive outcome, is linked to resilience, as it encourages perseverance and a willingness to confront challenges head-on.

Learning from past experiences is also crucial for cultivating resilience. Reflecting on how previous challenges were navigated, what strategies were effective, and what lessons were learned can provide valuable insights for dealing with future difficulties. This reflection enhances problem-solving skills, boosts confidence in one's ability to cope, and reinforces the belief that challenges can be overcome.

Finally, fostering a sense of purpose can significantly enhance resilience. When individuals have clear values and a sense of meaning in their lives, they are more motivated to persevere through difficulties. A strong sense of purpose provides a reason to keep going, even when faced with significant obstacles. Engaging in activities that are in line with one's values and contribute to a greater good can reinforce this sense of purpose and provide additional motivation to overcome challenges.

In conclusion, cultivating resilience in the face of challenges is a multifaceted process that involves adopting a growth mindset, building a supportive network, practicing self-care, setting realistic goals, maintaining a positive outlook, learning from past experiences, and fostering a sense of purpose. These strategies work together to enhance individuals' capacity to adapt to change, overcome adversity, and emerge stronger and more capable. Resilience is about surviving difficulties and thriving despite them, leading to personal growth, fulfillment, and a deeper appreciation for life's journey. By actively developing resilience, individuals can equip themselves with the tools required to navigate life's challenges with grace, determination, and optimism.

Building emotional intelligence habits

Building emotional intelligence (EI) habits is a transformative process that enhances one's ability to understand and manage emotions in oneself and others. Emotional intelligence, a term popularized by psychologist Daniel Goleman, encompasses a range of skills, including self-awareness, self-regulation, motivation, empathy, and social skills. Developing habits that bolster these aspects of EI can lead to strengthened relationships, better decision-making, and greater personal and professional success. This section explores strategies for cultivating EI habits, concentrating on practical steps individuals can take to enhance their emotional intelligence over time.

Self-awareness is the foundation of emotional intelligence. It involves recognizing and understanding one's emotions, triggers, and responses. One effective habit for building self-awareness is maintaining a daily journal. By reflecting on the day's events, emotions, and reactions, individuals can gain insights into their emotional patterns and triggers. This practice encourages introspection and mindfulness, helping individuals become more attuned to their internal emotional landscape. Additionally, setting aside time for meditation or mindfulness exercises can further enhance self-awareness by fostering a state of calm and focused attention on the present moment and one's feelings. Self-

regulation, the capacity to manage and regulate one's emotions, is another critical aspect of EI. Developing habits that promote self-regulation involves recognizing when emotions are beginning to escalate and employing strategies to moderate them. Techniques including deep breathing, counting to ten, or walking can help mitigate immediate emotional responses, allowing for more thoughtful and measured reactions. Another valuable habit is setting clear personal boundaries to prevent emotional exhaustion and maintain emotional balance. By understanding and respecting one's limits, individuals can better manage stress and avoid situations that disproportionately trigger negative emotions.

Motivation, particularly intrinsic motivation, is enhanced by setting and pursuing meaningful goals that align with one's values and interests. To build habits that foster motivation, individuals should practice setting specific, achievable goals and regularly reflecting on their progress and accomplishments. Celebrating small successes can boost morale and sustain motivation. Additionally, cultivating a positive outlook and visualizing successful outcomes can reinforce perseverance and resilience, critical components of intrinsic motivation.

Empathy, the capacity to understand and to share the feelings of others, is enhanced by actively practicing listening and perspective-taking. One habit to foster empathy is engaging in active listening during conversations, where the focus is entirely on understanding the speaker's perspective without immediately formulating a response. This practice demonstrates respect and care and deepens one's ability to comprehend and empathize with others' emotions. Additionally, seeking out and appreciating diverse perspectives can broaden one's empathetic understanding, encouraging a more inclusive and compassionate approach to interactions with others.

Social skills, like effective communication, conflict resolution, and relationship-building, are crucial for successfully navigating interpersonal dynamics. To develop these skills, individuals can practice expressing themselves clearly and assertively, using "I" statements to communicate feelings and needs without placing blame. Engaging in regular social activities and seeking opportunities for collaboration can also enhance one's social skills, providing a platform to practice and refine interpersonal interactions. Furthermore, participating in workshops or training focused on communication and teamwork can offer additional strategies and insights for developing effective social skills.

Building emotional intelligence habits requires consistent effort and a commitment to personal growth. It involves practicing specific techniques and adopting an overall mindset geared towards empathy, learning, and self-improvement. Feedback from others can be invaluable in this process, offering external perspectives on one's emotional responses and interactions. Seeking constructive feedback from trusted colleagues, friends, or mentors can provide guidance and encouragement for further development.

The benefits of cultivating EI habits extend beyond personal satisfaction and well-being. High EI is associated with better leadership, teamwork, and job performance in professional settings. Emotionally intelligent individuals are more adept at controlling stress, navigating workplace dynamics, and inspiring and motivating others. EI habits can lead to deeper connections, improved communication, and greater mutual understanding and support in personal relationships.

In conclusion, building emotional intelligence habits is a dynamic and rewarding journey that significantly impacts one's personal and professional life. By focusing on developing self-awareness, self-regulation, motivation, empathy, and social skills, individuals can enhance their ability to understand and manage emotions effectively. These habits not only improve interpersonal relationships and decision-making but also contribute to a fulfilling and successful life. As individuals become more emotionally intelligent, they are better equipped to face challenges, build strong relationships, and achieve their goals with resilience and understanding.

The lifelong journey of emotional growth

The journey of emotional growth is a lifelong process that involves continuously evolving and expanding our capacity to understand, express, and manage emotions. This journey is fundamental to personal development, influencing our relationships, resilience, decision-making, and overall well-being. Emotional growth encompasses the development of emotional intelligence (EI), including self-awareness, self-regulation, empathy, and social skills. This section explores the stages, challenges, and rewards of the lifelong journey of emotional growth, offering insights into how individuals can navigate this path with intention and mindfulness.

Emotional growth begins with self-awareness, the foundation upon which other aspects of emotional intelligence are built. Self-awareness involves recognizing and understanding one's emotions, identifying how they influence thoughts and actions, and acknowledging strengths and vulnerabilities. This stage requires introspection and honesty, as individuals must confront not only their positive attributes but also their flaws and insecurities. Cultivating self-awareness often involves reflecting on personal experiences, seeking feedback from others, and practicing mindfulness. These activities help individuals gain insights into their emotional patterns and triggers, setting the stage for further emotional growth.

As individuals become more self-aware, they embark on the process of self-regulation, learning to manage and control their emotional responses. This stage involves developing coping strategies for stress, anger, and other challenging emotions, such as deep breathing, meditation, or positive reframing. Self-regulation is crucial for maintaining emotional balance and making reasoned decisions, especially in high-pressure situations. It requires discipline and practice, as individuals must often override their instinctual responses to choose more constructive behaviors.

Empathy represents another critical dimension of emotional growth. It extends beyond simply understanding one's own emotions to include the ability to perceive and share in the feelings of others. Developing empathy involves actively listening to others, recognizing nonverbal emotional cues, and practicing perspective-taking. Empathy enriches interpersonal relationships, fostering deeper connections, and facilitating effective communication and conflict resolution. It also enhances compassion and understanding, enabling individuals to respond to others with sensitivity and support.

Social skills are also refined throughout the journey of emotional growth. These skills, including effective communication, teamwork, and conflict resolution, are essential for building and maintaining healthy relationships. Developing strong social skills involves learning to express oneself clearly and assertively, while also respecting the perspectives and boundaries of others. It also includes the ability to negotiate and compromise, recognizing that healthy relationships often require give-and-take. As individuals enhance their social skills, they improve their ability to navigate social dynamics, collaborate with others, and build supportive networks.

The journey of emotional growth is not linear; it involves cycles of progress, setbacks, and renewed efforts. Challenges such as personal loss, failure, or significant life changes can test and ultimately strengthen emotional resilience. These experiences provide opportunities for learning and growth, as individuals must adapt to new circumstances, reevaluate their priorities, and develop new coping mechanisms. The journey also involves unlearning negative emotional habits and beliefs that may have been internalized over time, a process that requires patience and self-compassion.

Throughout this journey, the role of external support cannot be overstated. Friends, family, mentors, and mental health professionals can provide guidance, encouragement, and feedback, helping individuals navigate their emotional development. Engaging in therapy or counseling can be particularly beneficial, offering a structured environment for exploring emotions, challenging negative thought patterns, and developing healthier emotional habits.

The rewards of the lifelong journey of emotional growth are profound. Individuals who invest in their emotional development enjoy improved mental health, stronger relationships, and greater life satisfaction. They are better equipped to handle stress, adjust to change, and face adversity with resilience. Emotional growth also enhances self-confidence and self-esteem, as individuals learn to value their emotional experiences and express themselves authentically.

In conclusion, the lifelong journey of emotional growth is a deeply personal and transformative process that shapes every aspect of an individual's life. It involves developing a nuanced understanding of oneself and others, managing emotions effectively, and building strong, healthy relationships. While challenges and setbacks mark the journey, they offer immeasurable rewards, including increased resilience, deeper connections, and a richer, more fulfilling life. By embracing this journey with openness, curiosity, and compassion, individuals can unlock their full emotional potential, leading to a life of greater balance, harmony, and joy.

CONCLUSION

As we reach the end of our journey through "EQ Blueprint: Navigating Emotions for Resilience and Connection," it's important to reflect on the profound impact that Emotional Intelligence (EQ) can have on our lives. Throughout these pages, we've explored the depths of EQ, uncovering its significance in shaping our personal and professional interactions, and empowering us to lead more fulfilling lives.

One of the key insights we've gained is that Emotional Intelligence is not just a set of skills to be learned; it's a lifelong journey of growth and self-discovery. From the foundational pillars of self-awareness and self-regulation to the essential qualities of empathy, social skills, and motivation, each aspect of EQ offers opportunities for deeper understanding and development.

But perhaps the most powerful lesson we've learned is that Emotional Intelligence is not just about managing our own emotions—it's about connecting with others on a deeper level. It's about recognizing the humanity in each person we encounter, and approaching every interaction with empathy, compassion, and understanding.

As we conclude our exploration of EQ, let us carry forward the lessons we've learned into our daily lives. Let us strive to cultivate greater self-awareness, regulate our emotions with grace and resilience, and forge deeper connections with those around us. And let us remember that the journey of Emotional Intelligence is not solitary; it's a journey we embark on together, supporting and uplifting one another along the way.

So, as you close the pages of this book, I invite you to continue your journey of Emotional Intelligence with an open heart and a curious mind. Embrace the challenges, celebrate the victories, and never stop seeking growth and connection. In the end, our capacity for emotional resilience and our ability to foster genuine connections truly define our success and fulfillment in life.

Thank you for buying and reading/ listening to our book. If you found this book useful/ helpful please take a few minutes and leave a review on the platform where you purchased our book. Your feedback matters greatly to us.